Being inside

268a

Onderzoek en beleid

Being inside

An explorative study into emotional reactions of juvenile offenders to custody

André M. van der Laan

Lisette Vervoorn

Coen A. van der Schans

Stefan Bogaerts

BJu | Boom Juridische uitgevers

Justitie Wetenschappelijk Onderzoek- en Documentatiecentrum

Onderzoek en beleid

De reeks Onderzoek en beleid omvat de rapporten van onderzoek dat door en in opdracht van het WODC is verricht.
Opname in de reeks betekent niet dat de inhoud van de rapporten het standpunt van de Minister van Justitie weergeeft.

Exemplaren van dit rapport kunnen worden besteld bij het distributiecentrum van Boom Juridische uitgevers:
Boom distributiecentrum te Meppel
Tel. 0522-23 75 55
Fax 0522-25 38 64
E-mail bdc@bdc.boom.nl

Voor ambtenaren van het Ministerie van Justitie is een beperkt aantal gratis exemplaren beschikbaar.
Deze kunnen worden besteld bij:
Bibliotheek WODC
Postbus 20301, 2500 EH Den Haag
Deze gratis levering geldt echter slechts zolang de voorraad strekt.

De integrale tekst van de WODC-rapporten is gratis te downloaden van www.wodc.nl.
Op www.wodc.nl is ook nadere informatie te vinden over andere WODC-publicaties.

ISBN 978 90 8974 012 0
NUR 741

Foreword

Rates of recidivism amongst juveniles who leave a correctional institution for juvenile offenders are high. As well as having a damaging effect on society, the behaviour of these juveniles causes a great deal of distress for victims, and the Ministry of Justice therefore feels that it is important to gain a better insight into the factors that can contribute to changing such behaviour. A lot of research is being carried out into interventions and their effectiveness. Hardly any attention has been devoted, however, to the experience of custody undergone by juveniles, the emotions that imprisonment evokes, and what effect emotions felt during custody have on recidivism. This study examines issues such as which characteristics of a custody or the social environment, and which characteristics of juvenile detainees themselves are related to the process of coping with imprisonment emotionally.

It is important to address this issue, as negative emotions have an inhibiting effect on a juvenile's ability to learn. The literature and discussions held with experts reveal, amongst other things, that juvenile detainees experience in particular the initial period of custody as emotionally stressful and that this period is associated with feelings of anxiety, shame, and guilt. For juveniles who have been in custody on remand, for example, this is a period of uncertainty. Levels of emotional stress will increase if juveniles receive conflicting reports from professionals with regard to the duration of their pre-trial incarceration.

At this point, I would like to thank the experts from four custodial institutions for their cooperation in this study. In addition, Prof Willem de Haan (University of Groningen) and Bas van Stokkom (Radboud University Nijmegen) made some valuable suggestions during the initial stages of the study. Finally, a word of thanks to Prof Ido Weijers (University of Utrecht), Loek Dijkman (Teijlingereind Correctional Institution for Juvenile Offenders), and Gert-Jan Terlouw (Youth and Crime Prevention Department, Ministry of Justice) for their assistance with this study.

Prof Frans L. Leeuw
Director of WODC
[*Wetenschappelijk Onderzoek- en Documentatiecentrum*, Research and Documentation Centre]

Contents

Summary

At the request of the Department for Judicial Youth Policy (DJJ) of the Ministry of Justice, the WODC (*Research and Documentation Centre*) conducted an exploratory study into the relation between incarceration and the emotional reactions of juveniles incarcerated in custodial institutions under criminal law. The background to this request relates to signals picked up during work visits to facilities that some young people respond to their custody with a reaction of pride. This reaction is undesirable; it will not stimulate the learning possibilities of juveniles with regard to behavioural change. In mutual consultation with DJJ, it was decided to interpret the request more broadly and to study various emotional reactions exhibited by juvenile offenders with regard to custody. The study was limited to the incarceration of juvenile offenders aged 12 to 24. Studies that relate to interventions or treatment during custody were excluded as much as possible. We also studied the literature regarding to the relation between emotional reactions felt during custody and recidivism.

Research question and method

The central question of the study is:
What is the relation between custody and the emotional reactions of juvenile inmates? And, based on the literature, what can be said about the effects of emotional reactions of juveniles during custody on criminal recidivism?

The central question is broken down into the following four research questions:

1. What differences exist with regard to individual characteristics of juveniles? We will focus specifically on differences in age, ethnic origin, and previous incarceration experiences.
2. What characteristics of the custody are related to the emotional reactions of the juveniles involved? This refers, e.g., to physical characteristics of detention, but also to whether the custody is experienced as fair, whether the young person feels that fair procedures are used in custody, or the phase of the custody the young person is in at that time.
3. What characteristics of the social environment are related to the emotional reactions of juveniles during custody? The term 'social environment' refers to the internal social environment, such as the group leaders, behavioural scientists, and fellow group members, as well as the external social environment, such as family members, friends, and external professional aid providers, such as lawyers, family guardians, or probation officers.
4. Is there an association between the emotional reactions during custody and recidivism according to literature?

We conducted two sub-studies. First, we carried out a literature study, for which we systematically searched a number of electronic databases. Secondly, we interviewed 21 experts who work in four different custodial institutions. This is an exploratory study, whereby it must be remembered that the findings cannot be generalised as though they were based on the opinions of all the experts employed in custodial institutions in the Netherlands. The literature study and the empirical study took place more or less simultaneously, which means that it was not possible to include all the aspects found in the literature study in the interviews. The results of the two sub-studies are described separately below. This summary does not provide literature references; for this, we refer to the report.

Judicial incarceration of juveniles and emotional reactions

Literature study
The literature study shows that little research has been done into the relation between incarceration and the way young people deal emotionally with this deprivation of liberty. Starting points were found mainly in studies based on the stress-coping perspective. In these studies, incarceration is considered a stressful experience, to which someone adjusts either adequately or inadequately. Adjustment to imprisonment is a process in which inadequate adjustment may be accompanied by emotional stress and behavioural problems. With regard to juveniles, the mainly Anglo-Saxon studies focus specifically on fear. More recently, limited studies have also been conducted into the relation between guilt or shame and incarceration.

First, individual characteristics of juveniles are relevant for their adaptation to imprisonment and the associated emotions. The studies found differences based on coping style and ethnic origin group, but there is less clarity with regard to age and previous experiences with the judicial authorities. See box S1 for a review of the findings.

Box S1 Individual characteristics and adjustment to custody (literature)

- Some coping styles are accompanied by strong emotional reactions during the custody (so-called 'emotional' and 'avoidance' coping styles). Such coping styles obstruct an adequate adjustment to the custody and, consequently, the functioning of the juvenile. Although changes in the coping styles appear to occur over time, it is not clear how this happens and whether or not these changes occur in every juvenile prisoner.

- The literature does find differences in the experienced emotions when it comes to the ethnic origin group. These are differences in the levels of fear, guilt, or shame. However, with regard to young people, there is insufficient information to be able to specify these differences by ethnic origin group.
- The literature does not allow for univocal pronouncements about age differences and differences between first offenders or recidivists when it comes to the emotional reactions of young people.
- The literature study also shows that prisoners with multiple problems experience more emotional stress and adjust to the custody less adequately than when such problems are lacking.

Secondly, the phase in custody relates to the extent to which the juvenile experiences feelings of fear, guilt, or shame. According to the literature, there is a process of adaptation to incarceration that has a number of sequential phases, in which the detainee experiences different emotional reactions. Other characteristics of a custody which, according to the literature, are connected to higher levels of fear, result in a refusal to participate in structured activities, like boot camp-style environments and disciplinary measures that are experienced as being unfair (see Box S2).

Box S2 Phases of adaptation to custody (literature)

- The initial period of imprisonment is a difficult one that, for many young people, is clearly accompanied by increased feelings of fear. Feelings of guilt and shame are also experienced more strongly in this period than during later stages of the incarceration.
- In the course of the incarceration, emotions that may be felt strongly at first become less intense and even occur less frequently. How long such periods last in individual juveniles is not clear, and depends in part on the personal situation.
- Juveniles may be very confused emotionally during the initial phase, but in the last phase juveniles should be able to adequately deal with the custody and experience fewer (emotional) problems with, for instance, rules, and the absence of loved ones or fellow group members than in earlier phases. This is a fragile process, throughout which the juvenile may revert to earlier phases for a number of reasons, such as kicking a drug habit, or a transfer to another department.

Third, the social environment is a relevant factor that helps juveniles to deal with their incarceration more adequately. However, the relation between the external social environment and the process of emotional adjustment to imprisonment is unclear. There is more clarity about the connection between emotional adjustment to incarceration and internal social support. A lack of internal social support is related to emotional stress, such as feelings of fear (emotions that may be the result of a lack of familiarity with incarceration and the structure of the regime).

The experts
In the interviews with experts, we asked to what extent they observed that characteristics of the incarceration, the social environment, and background characteristics of juvenile offenders in a custodial institution were related to six emotions, namely anger, guilt, shame, pride, remorse, and fear.

Box S3 In what extent are emotions of juveniles observed by experts (experts)

- According to the experts, the emotions anger, fear, and being proud of the committed offence occur frequently in boys in a custodial institution. The interviewed experts observed feelings of shame and guilt to a limited extent. Furthermore, according to the experts, the two emotions are difficult to distinguish. Remorse is rarely observed in incarcerated juveniles.

In the interviews, we investigated differences based on the background characteristics of the juveniles, namely age, ethnic origin, and previous experiences with the judicial authorities (see Box S4).

Box S4 Individual characteristics and emotional reactions (experts)

- According to the experts, hardly any differences based on age are observed in the various emotional reactions of juveniles, although feelings of pride occur somewhat more frequently in older boys, and feelings of fear and guilt in younger boys.
- To what extent differences in the emotional adjustment to imprisonment occur on the basis of ethnic origin is not clear. On this subject, there is no consensus among the experts, either.
- Finally, the experts observed differences between first-time offenders and recidivists, especially with regard to the experiencing of guilt, shame, and pride. Whenever the experts observed shame or guilt, this was more likely to occur in first-time offenders than in recidivists, whereas feelings of pride with regard to the committed offence are, in fact, observed slightly more often in recidivists. This may have something to do with age: first-time offenders tend to be younger than recidivists are.

Nearly all the experts observed boys who felt their incarceration was undeserved. This is associated with the institutions selected for this study. In custodial institutions, there are many boys who are still awaiting a decision about their criminal case (the boys who are on remand). It is, therefore, in their own best interest to maintain their innocence, and a proportion of these young people experience the remand as being disproportional to their offence. According to the experts, anger and shame are related to experiences of undeserved incarceration. See further box S5.

Box S5 Experiences of unjust custody (experts)

- Anger at the beginning of imprisonment is related to both uncertainty about one's criminal case, and the fact that some boys feel that they are not guilty and do not deserve an incarceration.
- A limited number of experts also observed that shame occurs more frequently in boys who experience their imprisonment as undeserved; this shame exists primarily because of the assumed reactions of the outside world. Boys who experience their imprisonment as undeserved are of the opinion that they are being stigmatised as a result.

In accordance with findings from the literature, the experts also observed that the duration of an incarceration is associated with emotional stress in juveniles (see Box S6). This relation between the duration and the emotional reactions, however, is not observed in all the boys. There are individual differences that are based, among other things, on personality, the committed offence, or previous detention experiences.

Box S6 Phases of custody (experts)

- Feelings of fear are more frequently observed in boys who have newly arrived in the institutions than in boys who have been there for longer.
- Feelings of shame and guilt are also mainly seen during the initial period (although these emotions are rarely observed).
- With regard to anger, there is no consensus on the question in which phase of custody it is more present.

Also in line with findings from the literature, the experts observed a clear connection between unfair treatment by group leaders and anger, but they did not see an association with feelings of guilt, shame, and fear. The latter observation does not correspond with findings from the literature. It is likely that those aspects of (un)fair treatment that we asked about in the interviews (whether a boy feels that he is being taken seriously and that people are listening to him) do not form part of any (un)fair treatment that is associated with feelings of fear.

In the interaction with incarcerated peers, group-dynamic mechanisms are central to emotional adjustment. In addition to 'standing up for one's interests' (for instance, anger is functional for protecting one's own interests) or 'prisonisation', the experts mainly observed general group processes such as obtaining 'status' or 'fear of ridicule'. These more general group mechanisms determine the hierarchy in the residential group.

Box S7 Incarcerated peers and emotional reactions (experts)

- Boys who want to obtain or maintain status in the residential group do so by reacting angrily to others, or by showing pride about their offence. These emotions were observed more frequently in recidivists than in first-time offenders.
- According to the experts, feelings of guilt and shame about the committed offence are shown rarely or not at all to fellow group members. One explanation may be that boys do not want to lose face in front of other boys ('fear of ridicule'); they do not want to appear to be the weaker party.

Emotions during incarceration and recidivism (literature)

The fourth research question concerns the relations between emotions experienced during incarceration and recidivism. We only used information obtained from the literature. A few studies have been conducted in which the relation was examined between the moral emotions anger, guilt, and shame experienced during custody and recidivism (see Box S8). These studies do not yet provide a clear picture.

Box S8 Emotions during incarceration and recidivism (literature)

- With regard to anger, the literature notes that the presence of this emotion during incarceration is not a good predictor for recidivism after detention.
- Some Anglo-Saxon studies show that feelings of guilt, evoked during restorative justice conferences, are predictors for reduced recidivism, while it cannot be said that feelings of guilt during custody are a determining factor, as so many other influences play a role in behaviour outside prison. Taking into account some of these other factors, a German study shows that feelings of guilt or shame in juveniles do not have a direct effect on recidivism, but that, when divided into subgroups, feelings of guilt in violent offenders are related to reduced recidivism. Because these findings are only based on a single study, little can as yet be said about the predictive value of, for instance, feelings of guilt in juveniles during incarceration in relation to recidivism.

Discussion and recommendations

The way an incarceration is experienced and the emotional reactions of juveniles incarcerated in a custodial institution do not remain constant throughout the entire period of imprisonment. The initial period, in particular, is emotionally stressful for juveniles. Some aspects that are associated with the emotional stress are described in the discussion.

The initial period of the custody is an emotionally stressful period
For juveniles in custody, there is considerable uncertainty about what their future holds in store, and certainly for those on remand this period is very unclear. The initial period is accompanied by (strong) feelings of fear. According to some studies, in the case of some young people it is accompanied by feelings of shame or guilt about what they have done and the consequences of their offence as well. The literature refers to a period of 'introspection', in which a form of increased awareness may be possible. The emotions experienced at the start of this period decrease as the juvenile is incarcerated for a longer period of time. In the Netherlands, no research has been conducted on the emotional adjustment of young people during the initial period of the incarceration, but the findings of the experts in our study correspond with those in the international literature. The experts observed that in some young people, more specifically in first-time offenders and young suspects, feelings of guilt about what they have done are observed more often at the start of the custody than in other young people.
If, in the case of specific groups of suspects, there is an initial period of introspection that fades as they are incarcerated longer, this initial period may be a more effective period to intervene and respond to the 'awareness-raising process' than in a later phase of the incarceration. For the moment, our study does not provide us with sufficient certainty to say that this applies to all first-time offenders and young suspects; for this purpose, a study conducted specifically among young people is needed.

Uncertainty and emotional stress during remand
Most juveniles start a judicial custody while being on remand. During this period, there is uncertainty about the course that the criminal case will take and, therefore, about the format and duration of the incarceration as well. From the point of view of criminal prosecution, remand is an important means that can be used during the prosecution phase. It may also be in the public interest to (temporarily) incarcerate juveniles when a prosecution is in progress. From a legal perspective, this remand is not a penalty, but the young people themselves experience custody as a punishment. While the incarceration during remand has its (legal and social) purpose, it also has undesirable side effects. According to the experts we interviewed, a substantial proportion of juveniles experience the imprisonment as unjust, or feel that the 'punishment' is disproportional. Although this may be a neutralisation of their own behaviour, this perception stimulates feelings of anger that may result in aggressive and/or rule-

breaking behaviour, with a greater chance of unsafe situations within the custodial institution.

Experienced injustice
Treatment that is perceived as being unfair can increase emotional stress (anger, fear) and might have a negative effect on the safety within a judicial institution. For this reason, it is important for staff working in correctional facilities to recognise situations that are perceived as being unfair, so that they can acquire a better understanding of the emotional stress of the juveniles concerned. One point that requires attention in this context is the contact between detainee and solicitor during the remand period. Comments from the various experts show that solicitors are not always aware of the emotional stress caused by the uncertainty of the custody during a remand period. This stress is enhanced by comments that imply that a young person's case will be decided in the near future, when the reality is ultimately quite different.

Based on the aforementioned discussion, we can make three recommendations:

Phasing of custody
The observation that the initial phase is emotionally stressful and may therefore increase the chances of problem behaviour also raises questions for the practice as to 'how to deal with this'. One possibility is to create residential groups in the correctional facilities based on phasing upon arrival (in some facilities this is already the case).

Preliminary residential plan during remand
A clearly described schedule for the custody, formulated right at the start, is an option for helping juveniles with their (emotional) adaptation to the incarceration. This may be achieved, for instance, by formulating a preliminary residential plan for all young people entering a custodial institution. A preliminary residential plan upon arrival can provide the juvenile with more certainty about his stay, while the evaluation of this plan provides insight into potential behavioural change. A preliminary residential plan may be based on an initial (remedial educational or psychological) screening of the juvenile, and may provide the basic definition for a training, education, and leisure programme. As a result of the inspection reports, the State Secretary of Justice recently emphasised in her letter to the Lower House of Parliament that such a screening is part of a reform process for correctional institutions for juvenile offenders. This screening 'at the gate' for the purpose of formulating a preliminary residential plan is not a task for the correctional institutions for juvenile offenders alone, but requires collaboration between different partners in the judicial chain. Such a screening should not be limited only to the

(criminogenic) risk factors, but should focus more broadly both on the needs of a juvenile and the ways in which a juvenile offender copes with stressful situations (coping styles). An early understanding of the coping styles of juveniles may provide the staff of correctional institutions for juvenile offenders with starting points on how to deal with specific young individuals, in order to reduce or prevent (imminent) emotional stress and related problem behaviour.

Univocal communication by all the parties involved about the course of the criminal case during the remand period
The emotional stress that is created by contradictory information about the young person's criminal case during the remand period, and the accompanying feelings of injustice should, in our opinion, be prevented as much as possible. We think it is relevant that solicitors are informed about the emotional stress caused by custody during a remand period. For this reason, we think it is important that the parties involved during the remand period provide the young people with univocal, consistent information. An important aspect of this is that, during this period, it is not clear what the court will decide.

1 Introduction

A large proportion of all young people who are committed to a custodial institution for juvenile offenders as a result of a criminal offence will come into contact with law enforcement again within a fairly short period of time. In the Netherlands, in the period 1997-2003, the percentage of young people being prosecuted for a criminal offence within two years after leaving an institution was between 54 and 60 percent (Wartna, Kalidien, Tollenaar & Essers, 2006). Explanations for persistent and/or serious delinquent behaviour, such as the risk and protective factors approach (see, for instance, Loeber, Slot, and Stouthamer-Loeber, 2006) focus either on the problems of the inmate involved, or those found in his immediate living environment. These are individual, familial, neighbourhood-, friends-, or school-related factors; hardly any attention is paid to the effects that detention experiences may have on recidivism. Other explanations, however, do refer to the influence of detention, or sanctioning in a more general context, on delinquency. Sampson and Laub (1993; Laub & Sampson, 2003) argue that detention is one of the links in a chain of disadvantages that increase the probability that someone will persist in offending. Persistence in offending is the result of cumulative disadvantage, and the experience of a detention is considered one of these disadvantages (Sampson & Laub, 1997). Detention weakens the offender's conventional social ties; for instance, as a result of the detention the person's ties with school or work become more difficult. This increases the probability of recidivism (Sampson and Laub, 1993; Laub & Sampson, 2003; see also Blokland, 2005). However, while Sampson and Laub (1993, 1997; and Laub & Sampson, 2003) focus on the effect of detention in general, they do not focus on the experiences of the offender undergoing the sanctioning. If we want to better understand the effects of detention on recidivism, we need insight into the 'black box' during the detention period: e.g. how it is experienced by inmates, what psychological (cognitive and emotional) and social problems detention causes, and what differences there are between inmates (Adams, 1992; Liebling & Maruna, 2005; Zamble & Quinsey, 1997).

In a letter from the Dutch Minister of Justice to the Lower House of Parliament, entitled 'New-style youth sanctions' (Ministry of Justice, 28 September 2004), it is suggested that if we want to understand recidivism in young people (and ultimately find reference points for reducing recidivism), it is not the offence we should use as the starting point. Rather, we should focus on the reaction of these young people to the sanction. A juvenile's reaction to a sanction not only relates to law-abiding behaviour after he has completed his punishment, but also relates to the adjustment to custody, *and* to the emotions associated with this situation. Experiences of anxiety, anger, or pride can reduce the potential of behavioural change of juveniles and can temper the effects of interventions (Van Binsbergen, 2003). In this study, we will focus specifically on the emotional reaction of juveniles to custody. Insight into this process will be of interest for correctional facilities for juveniles, not only for the detained youths, but also for staff members.

1.1 Research questions

The mainly international Anglo-Saxon literature on the adjustment of inmates to custody shows that the way in which, and the extent to which, inmates cope with detention is related to their functioning during and after the detention (Adams, 1992; French & Gendreau, 2006; Liebling & Maruna, 2005). In this process of adjusting to detention, emotions play an important role (Harvey, 2007; Lazarus, 2000; Liebling & Maruna, 2005; Zamble & Porporino, 1988). Empirical studies found an association between the stressful situation of being incarcerated and fear (Harvey, 2007; Liebling, 1999, 2006), or anger (see Loza & Loza-Fanous, 1999). These emotions, in turn, play a role in behavioural problems that may occur, such as aggressive behaviour (Thoch & Adams, 2002), self-harm (Harvey, 2007), (attempted) suicide (Liebling, 1999), or other behavioural problems (Loza & Loza-Fanous, 1999).

The transition to a detention situation is a stressful one (Bereswill, 2004; Harvey, 2007; Liebling, 1999; Mohino, Kirchner & Forns, 2002; Zamble & Porporino, 1988), that evokes a diversity of emotional reactions, such as shame, guilt, anger, or fear (see Harvey, 2007; Liebling, 1999; Liebling & Maruna, 2005; Nurse, Woodcock & Ormsby, 2003; Zamble & Porporino, 1988). From a functionalistic perspective on emotions, it is assumed that emotions are relevant in adjusting to (new) situations; they regulate cognitions and behaviour and vice versa (see Stegge, 2006). In order to deal adequately with the custody, it is important for inmates to be able to control their emotions. Inmates who are able to adjust to detention adequately will ultimately experience less psychological stress, have a higher self-esteem, and are more capable of interacting with fellow group members and group leaders, as well as with family members and friends, than inmates who do not adjust adequately (Harvey, 2007). Furthermore, research has shown that emotional stress reduces the motivation of juveniles for behavioural change (see Prochaska and DiClemente, 1994; in Van Binsbergen, 2003), so in order for judicial interventions to be effective, it is also relevant to reduce emotional stress and stimulate adequate coping with being incarcerated.
Adequate adjustment to detention is not only relevant for inmates. It also pertains to the functioning of those who deal with them directly: the staff members, the behavioural scientists, et cetera. During this period, inadequate adjustment to custody can manifest itself in, for instance, rule-breaking behaviour, aggression toward group leaders or fellow

inmates (French & Gendreau, 2006), withdrawn and isolated behaviour (Harvey, 2007), reduced self-esteem (Greve et al., 2001), depression, suicide attempts or suicide (Liebling, 1999), and problems in the interaction with family members or friends (Harvey, 2007). Thus, inadequate coping with custody and the associated emotional disturbances cause unsafe situations for both group members and staff members.

Emotional reactions of inmates are also associated with their functioning after their detention (Adams, 1992; Zamble & Quinsey, 1999; Zamble & Porporino, 1988). Within the perspective of research on the effects of moral emotions on behaviour, an occasional study indicates that 'dispositional' emotional reactions of inmates, measured during the custody, are linked to recidivism (Tangney et al., 2007; Loza & Loza-Fanous, 1999). Guilt, for instance, is associated with a smaller probability of recidivism (Tangney et al., 2007a; Tibbetts, 2003). Yet, in the case of juvenile offenders, the empirical results of longitudinal data are not always clear (Hosser, Windzio & Greve, 2005). From this moral emotions perspective, a few studies were conducted into the effects that shame and anger have on recidivism (see Hosser et al., 2005; Tangney et al., 2007a). A number of intervention programmes have actually been developed, – based, for the most part, on theoretical notions and studies among general (young) populations (for references see, for instance, Olthoff, 2002). In these programmes, the inmate is addressed with regard to, or made aware of, his or her feelings of guilt. This takes place in the context of the restorative justice conferences (Weijers, 2005; De Winter, Meijnen & Goldschmidt, 2005).
Empirical studies among young inmates, either on the connection between custody and emotions experienced during this period, or on the effects of the emotions during custody on recidivism, are generally rare (see Harvey, 2007; Liebling and Maruna, 2005; Tangney et al., 2007a). As far as we are aware, no research has been done into this topic in the Netherlands, although it would appear particularly relevant, both with regard to the short-term effects, – (problem) behaviour within the institution and the way in which group leaders deal with this –, and to the effects in the longer term, – the adjustment to a new situation after detention and recidivism.

At the request of the Judicial Youth Policy Department (DJJ), the WODC (*Research and Documentation Centre*) conducted an exploratory study into the relation between custody and the emotional reactions[1] of juveniles incarcerated in correctional facilities under criminal law. The interest of the DJJ is in the nature of the association and not in the extent to which the phenomenon occurs in the population of juvenile inmates. This

1 We will use the terminology of emotional reactions or emotional stress alternately.

means that insights are desired into possible backgrounds of the 'custody - emotional reactions' relation. In addition, for the DJJ, it is also important to know how and when emotional reactions are or may be influenced by, for instance, group leaders. The DJJ is also interested in differences that may exist among the subgroups of (incarcerated) young people, particularly among young people from different ethnic origin groups. Furthermore, the DJJ wants to know what reference points the literature offers for the connection between emotional reactions during detention and recidivism. Finally, this study does not look at young people who have been admitted to treatment clinics due to psychiatric problems.[2]

The central question of this study is twofold:

- *What is the relation between custody and the emotional reactions of juvenile inmates?*
- *Based on the literature, what can be said about the effects of emotional reactions of juveniles during custody on criminal recidivism?*

The central question is broken down into the following four research questions:

1. What individual differences exist in the emotional reactions of juveniles to custody? We will focus specifically on differences in age, ethnic origin, and previous incarceration experiences.
2. What characteristics of custody are related to emotional reactions of juvenile inmates? This refers, e.g., to physical characteristics of the detention, but also to whether the custody is experienced as fair, or whether the young person feels that fair procedures are being used in custody, and the phase of the custody the juvenile is in.
3. What characteristics of the social environment are related to the emotional reactions of juveniles during custody? 'Social environment' refers to the internal social environment, such as the group leaders, behavioural scientists, and fellow group members, as well as to the external social environment, such as family members, friends, and external professional aid providers, such as lawyers, family guardians, or probation officers.
4. Is there an association between the emotional reactions during custody and recidivism according to literature?

To answer the study's research questions, two sub-studies were conducted: a literature study and an empirical exploratory study based on interviews with experts. The first three research questions were the subject of both sub-studies. Research question four was only studied in the

2 Those with the strongest adjustment problems during deprivation of liberty are juveniles who have a psychiatric disorder (Adams, 1992; Toch & Adams, 2002). It is expected that, in this group, the emotional responses and coping styles during custody are associated more with their disorder than with the custody.

literature study. In Chapter 2, we will describe the method used for both studies in more detail. We will integrate the findings of both studies in the final chapter.

1.2 Demarcation of terms

Juveniles

Although we focused on juveniles who are minors under Dutch criminal law (aged between 12 and 17), during the study this demarcation proved difficult to maintain. In the first place, the few empirical studies into the topic also included older adolescents and young adults (aged between 18 and 24). Secondly, the experts also worked with youngsters older than 17 and, in their answers, would have young people in this older group in mind if they were a part of the group. In this study, the term 'juveniles' relates to minors under criminal law (aged between 12 and 17) as well as older adolescents and young adults (up to approximately age 24).

Custody in correctional facilities

Custody of juveniles relates to young people who are incarcerated in a custodial institution for juvenile offenders because of a criminal offence (in the Netherlands, until now, there are also correctional facilities for problematic youngsters who live there due to a problematic home environment). The study looks specifically at juveniles in custodial institutions and not at juveniles in treatment centres. Neither does this study look at the effects that specific interventions during the custody have on the emotional reactions of juveniles. For instance, this study does not look at the effects of restorative justice conferences on guilt among young inmates (for this type of study see, e.g., Daly, 2005; De Winter, Meijnen & Goldschmidt, 2005).

Emotions

The experience of being in custody can be accompanied by a variety of emotions. In the empirical part of the study, we will focus specifically on anger, shame, guilt, fear, pride, and remorse. This study is not the place for a detailed description of emotions and the effect of emotions within the judicial domain. For such a description, we refer the reader to the more specialist literature (see, for instance, Katz, 1999; Olthoff, 2000; Stegge 2006; Tangney et al., 2007b; Tibbetts, 2003; Weijers, 2000). However, five remarks about emotions are relevant in the context of this study.

First, every new situation, event, or experience engenders emotions to a greater or lesser extent. Emotions help someone to adjust to a new experience, either adequately or inadequately. In this context, they are also relevant with regard to custody. Contemporary (psychological) emotion

theories are based on a functionalistic perspective that emphasises the adaptive value of emotions (see, for instance, Stegge, 2006; Tangney et al., 2007b). Emotions allow a person to adjust to a changing environment. Emotions alert us to relevant situations and make us realise whether these situations are pleasant or threatening. Emotions make it possible for us to achieve goals. Fear, for example, is a response to a threat to an individual's safety and is engendered to allow the person involved to escape that threat. There are also moral emotions, which give an individual feedback on what is considered morally and socially acceptable. These are emotions like anger, guilt, shame, pride, or empathy. Feelings of guilt make someone aware that he/she has broken a moral rule, enabling him/her to take responsibility for this behaviour. Anger alerts a person to a threat to his/her interests and stimulates that person to eliminate the obstacles (Stegge, 2006). In short, from a functionalistic perspective, it may be asserted that emotions are important phenomena when it comes to (new) stressful or non-stressful situations or events (experiences).
Emotions are 'mechanisms of action' (Frijda, 1986; Tangney et al., 2007b). They drive various processes, such as attention, perception, memory, attributions, judgment, and behaviour. Between these phenomena, a complex interaction exists: emotions regulate cognitions and behaviour and, in turn, are influenced by cognitions and behaviour. Different types of emotions can also follow each other in quick succession, enhancing each other ('emotional links').

Second, psychological literature on emotions distinguishes between emotions that are mainly determined by a situation or specific event ('emotions as state') and emotional reactions as a disposition ('emotions as trait') (see Ferguson & Stegge, 1995; Stegge, Meerum Terwogt & Bijstra, 1998; Stegge, 2006; Tangney, 2007; Tibbetts, 2003). Emotions as state relate to an emotion that is the result of a specific experience (an event or experience someone is confronted with). The literature describes emotions as traits as affective styles that influence information processing, self-evaluation, and self-regulating behaviour over time and in different situations. In other words, an emotional disposition indicates how someone would generally respond emotionally in differing situations (Tangney, 2007b). An emotional disposition is not a characteristic of temperament; it is the result of experiences (Stegge et al., 1998). An accumulation of experiences will eventually lead to a dispositional affective style, and this style will subsequently influence someone's perceptions, interpretations, and behaviour (Fergusson et al., 1995: 181).
Emotions that are experienced as a result of custody do, in the first instance, mainly relate to emotions as 'state'. However, the emotional reaction during custody cannot be viewed separately from the way the juvenile inmate responds emotionally in general: his/her dispositional emotional response. Emotions that have been found to be related to

custody are, for instance, fear, anger, guilt, and shame. We will further describe the studies in which these emotions have been examined in relation to young people in Chapter 3. Research into the predictive value of emotional reactions for criminal recidivism focus mainly on variants of the emotions 'guilt' or 'shame' (Tangney et al., 2007b) and 'anger' (Loza & Loza-Fanous, 1999). In this context, we examined to what extent emotional dispositions are predictive for criminal recidivism. In Chapter 3 we will also look at the connection between dispositional emotions and recidivism.

Third, are there any age differences? Certain emotions, such as anger or fear, are observed in children at an early age (see, for instance, Lemeris & Dodge, 2000). As children grow older, they learn to handle such emotions (in either an adequate or an inadequate way). Other emotions develop over the course of someone's life; this is the case, for instance, with moral emotions like pride, shame, or guilt. These emotions can only be experienced if someone is able to picture how others view him and his behaviour. According to a functionalistic approach, such emotions follow a development pattern: during development, – from childhood via adolescence through to adulthood –, they take on different forms of expression and occur in differing levels of intensity (Mascolo & Fischer, 1995). Moral emotions gradually develop over extended periods of time and can ultimately take on complex forms, in which different emotions are linked together. As children get older, the emotions and the attributed cause of the emotions (one's own behaviour, 'self', or someone else) become increasingly complex, and the person grows more aware of this. In empirical studies, the age difference between children and young adolescents with regard to, for instance, shame, guilt, or pride has not (yet) been clearly demonstrated. Ferguson and Stegge et al. (2000a), for example, conducted a study into the relation between shame, guilt and pride, on the one hand, and the occurrence of the internalisation of problems among children at primary school age (8-13), on the other hand. The researchers compared a clinical group to a group of children from a primary school, both in the US. They did not find age differences with regard to shame (shame-proneness), guilt (guilt-proneness), and pride. It is possible that age differences do not become distinct until children and adolescents are compared to adults.

Fourth, what are the differences, if any, in the expression of emotions between men and women? Studies show that men often report more powerful externalising emotions, such as anger, than women, who tend to report less powerful externalising emotions, such as fear (Fischer et al., 2004). In general, men show more evidence of anger than women do. This is a universal pattern that is observed in a number of cultural contexts (Fischer et al., 2004). To what extent gender differences exist with regard

to the other moral emotions is less clear. With regard to shame and guilt, e.g., Ferguson, Eyre, and Ashbaker (2000b) studied this among college students. The literature they refer to shows that women are more vulnerable to shame than men and also experience shame more often. Ferguson et al. (2000b) studied this premise in a group of students aged between 18 and 28. They concluded that this gender difference might be based on a spurious association that depends on the context in which the person in question finds him or herself. Although their study showed that, on average, women did score higher on feelings of shame, this occurred precisely in those situations in which they were identified with behaviour or a person that was unwelcome to them. Men, by contrast, experienced more shame in situations that threatened their masculinity.
With regard to children and preadolescents, gender differences are less obvious. In a clinical group of children aged between 8 and 13, Fergusson et al. (2000a) did not find any differences between boys and girls with regard to shame, guilt, and pride. In children from the normal population, it became clear that boys tended a little more towards situational pride than girls. For this reason, to what extent custody will result in different emotions among boys or girls, is not easy to say at this stage. In this study we will limit ourselves to boys.

Fifth, experiencing and expressing moral emotions depends on the (expected) reactions of the social environment and the values that apply in the social context in question. Different studies show that there are cultural differences in the determinants at the foundation of moral emotions. Fischer et al. (1999) and Mosquera et al. (2000) observed cultural differences in pride, shame, and rage between cultures in which individual values take priority (the Dutch context) and cultures in which honour-related values take priority (the Spanish context). In the Spanish culture, honour-related values proved to be important triggers for pride, shame, and rage, whereas in the Dutch culture, individual values were important triggers. These findings imply that in cultural groups in which honour-related values are important (as is the case in the Moroccan and Turkish communities), a threat to such values will result in emotions of shame or anger more quickly than in other cultures, whereas reinforcement of these values will result in feelings of pride. In origin groups in which individual values are more prominent, such as the Dutch, emotions like shame or anger are more likely to be triggered by a threat to these individual values, whereas reinforcement of the individual values can trigger emotions like pride. To what extent there are differences between cultures with regard to age, gender, or education is not clear.
With regard to custody, we therefore can expect differences in the expression of emotions between young people of Dutch origin and young people from honour-related cultures. While native Dutch young people experience being in custody as a threat to individual values (a restricted

autonomy, no more contact with their family), in young people from honour-related cultures we can expect that their own honour, or that of their social environment, is/will also (be) threatened.

1.3 Juvenile custody in Dutch correctional institutions

In this paragraph, we will briefly describe the Dutch juvenile system, focusing specifically on custodial institutions. We will also look at the most notable differences between the Dutch and the Anglo-Saxon situation, because most of the literature described in the following chapters relates to the latter situation.

Pedagogical approach
The focal point of Dutch juvenile criminal law is the pedagogical approach in dealing with young people (see, for instance, Bartels, 2003; Weijers, 2001). This means that the emphasis is not only on general or specific prevention (see Dutch Ministry of Justice, 2006), but that care, education/rehabilitation, and resocialisation are central aspects of the approach as well. This pedagogic concept is reflected in the definition of the tasks of correctional facilities for juvenile offenders and is named as one of the explicit objectives by many juvenile correctional institutions (see, for instance, the websites of the various juvenile correctional facilities). Correctional facilities for juvenile offenders have three tasks:
1. to enforce a custodial sentence or custodial measure (the so-called PIJ measure, a custodial treatment order for juveniles);
2. the education/rehabilitation of the young person; and
3. preparing the young person for his return to society (resocialisation or re-integration into society). In addition, correctional facilities must provide juveniles of school age with an educational programme.

Correctional facilities for juvenile offenders
The Netherlands has 20 correctional facilities for juvenile offenders that accommodate young people in the age group between 12 and 17 (National Agency of Correctional Institutions (DJI), 2007). Adolescents in a higher age group (up to age 23) are also incarcerated in these institutions, because of, for instance, the personality of the perpetrator. Their incarceration might also depend on the circumstances under which the offence was committed (see De Jonge and Van der Linden, 2004). We make a distinction between treatment centres and custodial institutions. Treatment centres are for juveniles who have been given a PIJ measure, or for young people under a supervision order (OTS). The treatment centres focus on educating and treating young people with (serious) behavioural problems. The scope of this study does not allow us to look at young people

in treatment centres. In total, there are 14 custodial institutions in the Netherlands (DJI, 2007).

Custodial institutions
Custodial institutions are intended for young people on remand and young people who have been sentenced to juvenile detention. The custodial institutions also have accommodation for young people who are waiting to be placed in a treatment centre, juveniles awaiting a crisis placement, and juveniles in alien detention. In April 2007, there was room for 1,228 young people. The number of places per custodial institution ranges from 12 to 96 (DJI, April 2007).
The size of the population in a custodial institution fluctuates throughout the year. Throughout 2006, the custodial institutions accommodated a total of 5,862 young people.
According to the National Agency of Correctional Institutions (DJI), in 2006, 43.3% of these cases involved placement under a supervision order (OTS), 35.7% of the young people in correctional institutions were there on remand, 9.6% were there under a PIJ measure, and 7.0% under juvenile detention. In addition, 3.6% were in alien detention and 0.7% of all cases were guardianship cases.
Boys and girls are housed separately (art. 13 of the Youth Custodial Institutions (Framework) Act). In 2006, more than three-quarters of the population of young people in custodial institutions were boys (DJI, August 2007). The minimum age of young people who are incarcerated under criminal law is 12. An overview from the DJI (August 2007) shows that, in 2006, the majority of young people in custodial institutions were aged 16 and 17 (52.8%), followed by young people aged 14 and 15 (28.6%). Slightly more than one in every ten young people in custodial institutions were 18 or older (13.7%) and nearly one-fifth of all young people (4.8%) were younger than 14. In 2006, the origin of four out of every ten young people was Dutch (39.4%). With regard to the young people of foreign heritage, most came from families of Moroccan origin (15.0%), followed by those of Surinamese origin (9.2%). The largest group of young people of non-Dutch origin consisted of young people who originated from other non-Western countries, namely 22.6% (DJI, 2007).

Fluctuation in juveniles in custodial institutions
There is a large turnover of young people in correctional institutions. For young people on remand, it is not yet clear what sanction or measure they will be given – it is even possible that they may be acquitted. For these young people it is not known how long their stay will be, when they will be summoned to appear and what the sanction will be. The majority of all young people on remand (75%) go home, on average after only 30 days (see also Matkoski & Verveacke, 2007).

Phasing
When young people are incarcerated in a custodial institution, their stay might be phased. For new arrivals, there is a different daily programme than for young people who have been in the correctional institution for some time. Initially, juveniles will spend more time in their own room so they can take their time to get used to the institution, the group leaders, the other juveniles, the programme, and the rules. This initial phase is also used to evaluate for which group the juvenile is best suited. If possible, the juvenile will participate in the educational programme right from the start. After the initial familiarisation phase, the young people can fully participate in all the activities with their own age group. There is no general guideline for the duration of this initial phase.

Residential plan
For young people entering a correctional institution for juvenile offenders, a 'residential plan' is formulated (art. 20 Bjj). Among other things, this plan describes the objectives on which the young person must work during his stay. These objectives can vary from learning practical skills to receiving training. This residential plan is formulated for young people who will be in the institution for an extended period of time. It is normally not formulated until the young person has been in the custodial institution for several weeks, as a residential plan is only compulsory for young people with a residual sentence of three months (art. 20 Bjj). This means that a large proportion of all residents in a custodial institution, especially those on remand, will not be eligible for a residential plan (see also Matkoski & Verveacke, 2007).

Residential group
In a custodial institution, a young person is placed in a so-called 'residential group' (art. 22 of the Youth Custodial Institutions (Framework) Act). The number of residential groups per correctional institution depends on the capacity. Young people are placed in groups with a maximum of twelve per group. In exceptional cases, young people are not placed in a group (art. 22 of the Youth Custodial Institutions (Framework) Act), for instance in case of a limited stay in a start unit, or when the person involved is excluded because of personal factors. In practice, some correctional institutions for young offenders arrange to have young people spend their first week partially in their own room, which limits their contact with the groups (internal rules Teylingereind, 2007). This allows them to get used to being incarcerated and helps determine which group in the institution is most suitable for the young person. Initially, they will also have a different daily programme. Once again, there is no general guideline for the duration of this familiarisation phase.

In some custodial institutions, boys in the same age group are housed together (for instance, a group for under-16s, and a group for over-16s)[3]. Other correctional institutions structure their groups based on the destination plan of the young people (for instance an intake group, an observation group, or a special care group[4]), which does not allow for the creation of groups with young people of the same age.

Own room
In the Netherlands, juveniles in correctional institutions get their own room. These rooms are used at times when the young people are not in their residential group. These are private rooms containing a bed, a toilet, washing facilities, a mirror, a wardrobe/bookcase, and often a desk. Within certain limits, the young people are allowed to bring private possessions with them, to keep in their rooms. By means of a hatch in the door, the staff can check on the young person and, if necessary, staff members can also enter the room.

Daily programme
In the custodial institutions, the young people have a fixed daily programme. Important components of the programme are 'quiet, order, regularity and structure'. The young inmates have breakfast, lunch and dinner in a group. As long as they are of school age, they will attend school in the institution. After school and on weekends, they have the option of spending some time in the residential group's shared living room. The living room is used for leisure activities and joint meals. The inmates also have the option to exercise, hang out, talk, et cetera, in the outdoor recreational area, which is enclosed by high-quality security fences around the sides. At night, the young people stay in their own, – locked –, rooms.

Group leaders
During the day, when the young people conduct their activities 'in the group', group leaders are also present. The minimum number of group leaders is two. The minimum performance level of the group leaders is MBO (*Intermediate Vocational Education*), although this is not the minimum educational level required. According to many institutions, the group leaders are not as well educated as would be desirable. A study by the National Auditor's Office (2007) into the functioning of custodial institutions and treatment centres shows that one quarter of the group leaders do not have a sector-oriented professional education, and that half perform on MBO level, whereas the institutions themselves feel that they would achieve better results with employees who have an education on HBO level (*Higher Vocational Education*).

3 See, for instance, custodial institution De Hunneberg.
4 See, for instance, custodial institution and treatment centre Teylingereind.

In most institutions, group leaders act as a mentor to at least one young person. The mentor is the first point of contact for the young person in question as well as for those involved in the young person's care, such as parents, professional aid providers, solicitors, et cetera. To what extent this extra role can be guaranteed in practice is unclear, because of the lack of stability in the number of group leaders responsible for looking after the young people, This was shown in the report of the National Auditor's Office (2007), based on a random test of treatment centres and custodial institutions.

Contact with the outside world
Young people in a custodial institution can stay in touch with the outside world in a number of ways. This contact is regulated by law and may consist of mail, personal visits, or telephone calls. Parents are given the opportunity to have frequent contact with their child. In line with the Youth Custodial Institutions (Framework) Act, young people must be given the opportunity to receive a visitor from outside the institution for a minimum of one hour a week (art. 43 of the Youth Custodial Institutions (Framework) Act). A distinction is made between 'privileged' visitors, such as professional aid providers and also parents, and 'non-privileged' visitors (other family members or friends). The first group has broader visiting options, more than once a week. This is left to the institutions themselves. At least twice a week, children can also make telephone calls to people outside the institution (art. 44 of the Youth Custodial Institutions (Framework) Act). Again, in some institutions, privileged persons may be called whenever necessary.

International perspective
Although in the Anglo-Saxon countries and the Netherlands alike, juveniles in the age group between 12 and 17 have a special place within the judicial system, there are also clear differences between the countries, both with regard to the number of youths in custody and the way in which they are incarcerated in correctional institutions for young offenders. An important difference can immediately be seen in the underlying ideology. In the US, the resocialisation of young inmates is an important point, but the custody is still mainly viewed from angle of punishment and incapacitation, for the purpose of protecting society (Weijers, 2007).
The situation in Dutch custodial institutions differs from those in the US and Great Britain, as well. There are differences in, for example, the composition of the population, the size of the institutions, the staff-inmate ratio, the type of accommodation for the young people, the residential group, and the educational level of the group leaders (e.g., see Neustater, 2002; OJJDP, 2006). The Dutch situation differs most from that in America. Both in the US and in Great Britain, the correctional institutions for juvenile offenders are, on average, larger than those in the Netherlands (see,

for instance, Sickmund, 2002; Snyder et al., 2006). The staff-inmate ratio in the Anglo-Saxon countries is also much higher than in the Netherlands. Whereas custodial institutions in the Netherlands have an average of two to three group leaders per group of twelve young people (1:6 – 1:4), in Great Britain the staff-inmate ratio in the Young Offenders Institutions is 1:10 (Youth Justice Board, 2007). The use of cells for more than one person also proves to be more rule than exception in the US and, to a lesser extent, in Great Britain. In the Anglo-Saxon countries, single-person cells for young people are mostly used for those who exhibit problem behaviour (see Boendermaker et al., 2006).

1.4 Reading guide

This report describes the results of two sub-studies into the relation between judicial custody and the emotional reactions of juveniles to it. In the second chapter of this report, we will describe the research methods used in both sub-studies. The literature study is described in Chapter 3. We will describe the empirical findings from the – mainly international – literature relating to the determinants for young people's adjustment to custody and the emotions that are relevant in this context. Furthermore, we will look at empirical studies that establish a link between emotions observed during detention and recidivism after detention. Part two of this study relates to an empirical study among experts employed in four correctional institutions for young offenders in the Netherlands. In Chapters 4, 5 and 6, we will report the findings from these interviews. Finally, Chapter 7 will provide some concluding remarks.

2 Method

This chapter describes the methods used in both studies. We distinguish a literature study and an empirical study, for which a number of experts in different custodial institutions were interviewed.

2.1 Literature study

The purpose of the literature study was to clarify the connection between custody and emotional reactions among adolescent and young adult inmates, using (inter)national empirical studies. In this study, we combined a systematic search strategy of electronic databases with a snowball method for literature research.

The databases
To gather the literature, the databases of the researchers themselves were consulted and a number of scientific literature databases (WODC library database, Picarta, ISI Web of Knowledge, PsychINFO, NCJRS, Ingenta and Google.scholar) were systematically searched. While searching these databases, we linked a number of combinations of keywords relating to detention or judicial punishments to the different types of emotions. In the first instance, we selected a broad range of literature. To get the most comprehensive overview of the literature relating to custody, the following keywords were used: 'detention', 'judicial punishment', 'sanction', 'inmates', and 'custody' or variants thereof (see appendix 2). With regard to emotions we selected, in the first phase, the broadest possible angles and used the following keywords: 'shame', 'humiliation', 'guilt', 'remorse', 'empathy', 'anger', and 'fear'.

The systematic research of the databases resulted in a great deal of literature concerning psychological and therapeutic interventions during custodial sentences. These studies focus specifically either on the effects of interventions on inmates' well-being during or after the detention, or on the recidivism of inmates. As this study does not deal with the effects of interventions, these studies were not included. After removing the research in question, it became clear that there are few studies that focus specifically on the connection between custody and emotional reactions of juveniles, and that there are hardly any studies dealing with research into the relationship between emotions during custody and recidivism after detention.
However, we did find indications that in studies in which 'coping with' or 'adaptation to' detention was the main point, the emotional reactions of young people were also studied indirectly. For this reason, the literature databases were searched once more for studies in which coping with or adaptation to detention is studied.

In addition to the systematic search method, we used a snowball method, in which both the literature references found during the systematic search, and the literature references that the researchers already had were used as the starting point.
We also interviewed three scholars who are experts in this field. In addition to useful suggestions about the direction the literature study should take, they also suggested specific literature.

Literature selection and analysis
Next, the literature relevant to answering the first three research questions was filtered on the basis of abstracts. We used the studies that related to 1) incarceration, 2) the emotions engendered as a result of the incarceration and 3) juveniles (up to the age of 24). Studies relating to the psychiatric problems of young inmates were excluded as much as possible.
In addition, we checked which literature from the earlier search focuses on the connection between emotions during detention, and recidivism. This search revealed that little research has been done on this subject matter. We therefore decided to adopt a broader angle when it came to answering the fourth research question, and also to focus on literature regarding adults. We will say more about this in Chapter 3.
For the analysis of the literature, we used a variant of the so-called *narrative review* (see, for instance, Weerman et al., 2006; Welsh & Farrington, 2006). This means that the separate studies are carefully described first. Next, the results are arranged on the basis of the research questions. We chose this method because the greater part of the studies we reviewed is based mainly on qualitative research.

2.2 Interviews with experts

The purpose of the empirical study is to clarify the connections discerned between (aspects of) custody and emotional reactions for the Dutch context of the correctional institutions for juvenile offenders. As far as we are aware, no empirical research into the relation between custody and emotional reactions in juveniles in correctional institutions for juvenile offenders has been conducted in the Netherlands. Since the representativeness of the sample is not the objective of this study, a qualitative study is more appropriate. We opted for an exploratory empirical study among experts who are in daily contact with young male inmates. A qualitative study method, the semi-structured interview, was used.

The expert group
The experts were group leaders and behavioural scientists in correctional institutions for juvenile offenders, more specifically custodial institutions. Using these people as participants in the study made it possible

to acquire, within a limited period of time, an understanding of the emotions observed in young inmates, as well as the determinants for these emotions. More specifically, we asked, for instance, whether the group leaders observed differences based on origin, criminal history, and duration of the detention. By interviewing group leaders, it was possible to obtain information regarding different subgroups in a relatively short period of time, without having to interview large numbers of young inmates.

A total of 17 group leaders and 4 behavioural scientists (psychologists and remedial educationalists) from four correctional institutions for young offenders in the centre, the west and the south of the Netherlands were interviewed.
Nine of the seventeen group leaders were women, and eight were men. With regard to the behavioural scientists who were interviewed, two were women and two were men.
Of nineteen of the experts, the following information is known: their age, the average duration of their work experience in custodial institutions, their origin, and their educational level. The average age of the experts was 35.5 (range 24-57), while on average the group leaders were a little younger than the behavioural scientists (33.1 and 44.8 respectively). On average, they had worked in the field of juvenile law for 8.7 years (range 8 months – 30 years). Here, too, the rule applied that, on average, the group leaders had been working in correctional institutions for young offenders for a shorter period of time than the behavioural scientists (6.5 and 17 years respectively). The majority of the experts were of Dutch origin (N=16), while of the remaining three, two were of Antillean origin and one of Moroccan origin. The educational level of the group leaders ranged from MBO (*Intermediate Vocational Education; N=8*) to HBO (*Higher Vocational Education; N=7*). The behavioural scientists all have an academic degree. Both group leaders and behavioural scientists were interviewed; hereafter, we will also refer to them as 'experts'.

Young people are held in custodial institutions for different reasons (see paragraph 1.4). The answers of the experts related to young people on remand, young people in juvenile detention, or young people in alien detention. In view of the method we used, it is not possible to separate these groups; to do so would require further research involving the juveniles themselves.

The semi-structured questionnaire
The experts were interviewed on the basis of a semi-structured questionnaire (see appendix 2 for the questionnaire). Semi-structured interviews make it possible to look more closely at the answers of the experts in a fixed pattern. Because all the experts were asked the same questions,

the comparability of the interviews was increased. The semi-structured nature of the interview also makes it possible to delve more deeply into specific situations and to ask for reasons. This makes it possible to clarify possible associations about which little is known. Prior to the interviews, the questionnaire was tested on both a group leader and a behavioural scientist. Based on this test, a number of adjustments were made to the formulation of the questions.

The interviews were conducted in the period from 9 January 2007 up to and including 20 February 2007. The interviews with group leaders and behavioural scientists were recorded with a *voice recorder* and typed up integrally. Next, the answers of the group leaders were categorised per research question and per emotion, whereby we specifically noted what the group leaders told us with regard to the relationship between emotions and factors from the diagram below (see Figure 1).

The interviews centred on the emotions anger, shame, guilt, pride, fear, and remorse. For each of these emotions, questions were asked that can be classified into three domains. These domains, which were used for the analysis of the interviews, are the following: a) individual characteristics of the young people, b) characteristics of deprivation of liberty, and b) the (internal and external) social environment.
First, we asked whether the experts observed differences in the emotional reactions of young inmates on the basis of background characteristics. More specifically, these characteristics concern differences in age, origin, and previous experience with the judicial authorities.
Secondly, we examined whether or not characteristics of custody appear to be related to the different emotions. For each emotion, we checked whether the experts observed a relationship between the phase of the custody and the (perceived) fairness of the custody. With regard to the duration of the stay in the correctional institution for juvenile offenders, we asked about the difference between new arrivals and those who have been in the institution longer, and the associated emotions. In this context, the fairness of the custody relates to differences between boys who feel that they are being sanctioned deservedly, and boys who feel that they are not.
Third, we assessed whether the social environment was associated with the emotional reactions of the young people. This concerns the internal and external social environment. We asked the experts to what extent the relationship between the emotional reactions of young people and the custody is influenced by the treatment received from group leaders and by the interaction with fellow group members (the internal social environment). With regard to the interaction with group leaders, we asked whether there is a specific emotion among the boys that is associated with being taken seriously, and with the group leader's showing respect and listening

to the boys (a 'fair' treatment). We also asked whether the experts noted any effects related to the external social environment, such as parents.

An interview in which all the aspects of every emotion for every domain were discussed would be too time-consuming for the experts. We therefore decided to only question every aspect with regard to the emotions anger, shame, and guilt. With regard to the emotions pride, fear, and remorse we asked the experts to indicate, on a more general scale, whether or not they observed these aspects in the various emotions.

Figure 1 Schematically outlines the various domains

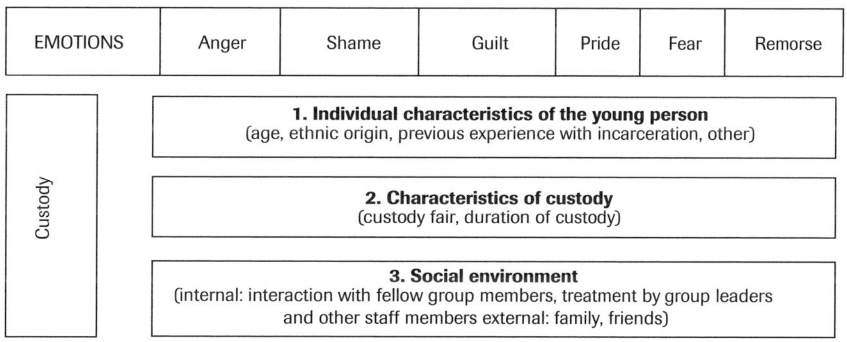

Study 1: Literature study

3 Custody and emotional reactions

The transition to a custodial situation is a stressful event. Juveniles are faced with a new environment, in which they are restricted in their freedom and autonomy. They are faced with an enforced daily structure that differs from their normal daily routine at home, and they are forced to share their new situation with others they do not know. It is to be expected that a custodial situation will engender strong emotional reactions. Certainly initially, as the young people are separated from their familiar environment and are only allowed to see family members and friends at prearranged times. The stressful experiences demand a lot of the juveniles and are associated with adjustment problems that, in some, manifest themselves as behavioural and psychological problems. Some of the young inmates also have existing psychological problems that make the adjustment to a custodial context even more difficult.
In this chapter, we will describe the research questions on the basis of the (inter)national literature. We will start the chapter with a description of a number of perspectives on the basis of which the study on adjustment to detention is structured (paragraph 3.1). The three subsequent subparagraphs then describe the – mainly international – empirical studies that focus on the connection between custody and emotional reactions of juveniles (paragraph 3.2). Paragraph 3.3 deals with empirical studies on the relation of emotional reactions during incarceration and recidivism. To conclude, paragraph 3.4 presents a brief summary of the findings.

3.1 Perspectives on adjustment to custody and emotions

According to the review study of Adams (1992), in recent decades, the research into the way inmates adjust to their custody has been initiated from four different perspectives that more or less succeeded one another over the course of time. Early studies focused on 'prisonisation', followed by research in which models of 'importation' and 'deprivation' were studied. Since the Eighties, studies on custody have been conducted from the interactionistic and stress-coping angles that were more or less complementary, More recently, we have seen a focus on the effects of the perceived fairness (of rules and procedures) on the way in which inmates handle the deprivation of liberty. Research based on these different perspectives has resulted in insights concerning both the determinants of adjustment to custody and the associated emotions. Before we look at these empirical insights more closely, we will clarify the different perspectives in this paragraph.

Prisonisation
Studies into the adjustment to detention conducted in the Fifties and Sixties focused mainly on the social organisation and culture of the inmate population and on the unique characteristics of prisons as organi-

sations. Theoretical perspectives emphasised the importance of the solidarity found by inmates in the 'inmate code', a social manner that is characterised by norms like non-cooperation and resistance against staff members. New inmates supposedly adopted this attitude quickly and the resistant attitude was regarded as a functional form of adjustment to the incarceration. This process was referred to as 'prisonisation' (Clemmer, 1958; in Adams, 1992). In early studies based on the prisonisation perspective, little attention was given to the emotional adjustment to custody and the psychological suffering of inmates. The emphasis was mainly on the attitudes and values that apply in a prison culture (Adams, 1992).

Importation, deprivation and situational models

Poor attention for the personal characteristics of inmates and the vagueness of the 'prisonisation' concept were important criticisms that resulted in new perspectives in the research on the adjustment to detention, according to Adams (1992: 279). In the Sixties and Seventies, new theoretical perspectives concerning the adjustment to detention were formulated with the 'importation' and 'deprivation' models.

Based on the importation model, researchers argued that characteristics of individuals that already exist prior to the deprivation of liberty, such as someone's criminal history, ethnic origin group, and characteristics of the family, determine how they adjust to detention and what behaviour they will exhibit. In other words, inmates 'import' the risk factors from their daily life into the detention situation. By contrast, based on the deprivation model, researchers argued that the dominant factor that impedes the adjustment to custody is the restrictive climate of the custody itself. According to this model, the detention environment, in which every type of institution and every type of activity through to the number of inmates and the physical structure were thrown together collectively, determines to an important extent the way in which inmates adjust.

Although the models were considered to be diametrically opposed, empirical support has been found for both, and contemporary researchers conclude that both importation and deprivation processes are involved in the adjustment to detention (see, for instance, Gover, MacKenzie & Armstrong, 2000). Based on empirical research, it is now also believed that individual inmates react differently to custody (Adams, 1992: 280). Contemporary research into importation and deprivation factors among inmates has provided some insights into the emotional reactions of inmates, such as feelings of fear, and the determinants for these reactions (see, for instance, the study by Gover et al., 2000, referred to later in this chapter).

In the Nineties, a third model was added: the situational model (see Jiang et al., 2002). This model assumes that situational factors such as the season, the location, or the complex relationship between staff and inmates are important factors contributing to the way in which inmates adjust to detention.

Interactionism

From an 'interactionistic' perspective, it is assumed that the environment influences the behaviour of individuals because the demands that the environment imposes on individuals are – or are not – compatible with someone's individual (psychological) orientation. Physical aspects of the environment are relevant in this context but, according to Adams (1992), research among inmates has focused mainly on the socio-psychological dimensions of the environment to which an individual must adapt. Some situations are regular and predictable; others are characterised by safety and support, whereas yet other situations emphasise freedom, autonomy, and self-expression. These characteristics of the environment are separate from the characteristics of a person. The chances of adjustment problems increase if the person and the environment are not compatible; adjustment problems may be prevented or overcome by looking for this compatibility (Adams, 1992).

'Stress-coping'

A second perspective that was introduced to prison studies at the end of the Eighties and the start of the Nineties was that of the 'stress-coping' model. Studies that focus on this model investigate the practical, social, and psychological adjustment of inmates to custody (for overviews see Adams, 1992; Harvey, 2007). In general, the main research question in these studies comes down to 'how and under what circumstances do inmates adjust to their incarceration?' In those studies in which psychological adjustment to custody is studied, the emotional reactions of inmates, such as fear (Harvey, 2007; Liebling, 1999; Liebling & Matsueda, 2005; Zamble & Porporino, 1988) or anger (Zamble & Porporino, 1988) are also discussed.

More generally speaking, studies based on the 'stress-coping' perspective (Lazarus, 2000) focus on the psychological aspects (both cognitions and emotions) of adjustment to stressful experiences. Whether an experience is considered stressful or not, and what the subsequent reactions to this experience are, depends on the way in which someone views this experience ('appraisal') and deals with it from a cognitive, emotional, and behavioural point of view. Adjustment to a stressful experience is viewed as a process in time. If a person adjusts adequately to the stressful experience concerned, stabilisation of cognitions, emotions and behaviour will be the result (an 'equilibrium', see for instance Harvey, 2007, later in this chapter). Inadequate adjustment is accompanied by an increase in (emotional) tension in the short term (Lazarus, 2000), as indicated by the expression of strong emotions (anger, fear, depression), a decline in psychological well-being, and the emergence of behavioural problems. In the longer term, negative effects on someone's (psychological) health, well-being, or social functioning may become evident (see Lazarus, 2000: 201).

Procedural Justice

Recently, the studies into the adjustment to custody among adult inmates have also started looking at fairness in relation to the adjustment to incarceration, and more specifically the extent to which fair treatment by staff members is linked to feelings of e.g. fear among inmates (Harvey, 2007; Liebling, 2006). In some studies based on the deprivation model, fairness of punishment in incarceration was one of the determinants for the adjustment to custody (see, for instance, Gover et al., 2000). In the contemporary studies, fairness is looked at from the 'procedural justice' perspective (Tyler, 1991; 2003), in which fairness of the treatment provided by staff members such as group leaders is the focal point (Harvey, 2007; Liebling, 2006).

The relationship between fair treatment and sanctioning in general is the focal point of the so-called procedural justice perspective (see Lind & Tyler, 1988; Tyler, 1990; 2003). Research based on this perspective focuses on the question why people obey the rules and, more specifically, why people who are/have been involved with law enforcement agencies (the police, the courts) obey the rules. The central issue is the extent to which someone experiences a sanction to be fair and the extent to which he or she feels he/she is being treated fairly by the law enforcement agents. In this context, fair treatment is operationalised in terms of (e.g.) 'listening to someone', 'showing respect', or 'taking someone seriously' (see, for instance, Tyler, 1990; Van der Laan, 2004). According to Tyler (1990; 2003), the fairness of treatment is more important than the fairness of a sanction (whether a sanction is justified, or whether the severity of the sanction is appropriate to the seriousness of the offence). The more someone feels he/she is being treated fairly, the sooner he/she will acknowledge the legitimacy of the law enforcement agents and consequently start obeying the rules. Unfair treatment, by contrast, is related to reducing the experienced legitimacy of law enforcement and reduced preparedness to comply with the rules.

We are not aware of any studies on the relation between the perceived fair treatment by staff members or group leaders and the emotional reactions of juvenile inmates. This is remarkable for a number of reasons. Firstly, adjustment to custody depends to a considerable extent on how the quality of the relationship with group leaders is experienced, which includes the perceived fairness of the treatment (see Biggam & Power, 1997; Harvey, 2007, in paragraph 3.3). In addition, population studies and research among suspects arrested by the police shows that people who feel they are being treated fairly find it easier to acknowledge the legitimacy of persons in authority, and are therefore more likely to comply with the rules, than people who feel they are being treated unfairly (Tyler, 1990; Paternoster et al., 1997). Particularly in the case of custody, this finding appears to be important, making possible the discovery of reasons for adjustment problems during incarceration.

3.2 Individual characteristics, characteristics of custody and of social environment

As mentioned before, we have found little research in which the emotional reactions of *juvenile* inmates have been examined directly. However, studies from the stress-coping perspective focused indirectly on the emotional reactions of juvenile inmates, like, for instance, fear. In a few other studies, anger, shame, or guilt among incarcerated juveniles have also been studied. First, we will describe empirical studies that show individual differences in emotional adjustment of juveniles to being incarcerated (research question 1). Next, we will describe empirical studies that have focused on the characteristics of incarceration in relation to emotional reactions (research question 2). Finally, we will mention empirical studies that have focused on the social environment in relation to emotional adjustment (research question 3).

First, some methodological remarks are in order about the limits of our conclusions. A few studies have used longitudinal designs in order to find effects of incarceration on (emotional) adjustment. However, most studies we found on this topic used cross-sectional designs, which limits the conclusions to a mere association. Besides, different ways have been used of operationalising the central constructs, resulting in difficulties with the mutual comparison of the empirical studies. Because of these limitations, we are unable to draw firm conclusions about the effects of individual differences, incarceration, or social environment on the emotional adjustment of juveniles to detention.

3.2.1 Individual characteristics

In his review, Adams (1992) mentions that those inmates who adjusted most inadequately to incarceration and experience high levels of emotional stress are those who had a history of psychiatric problems. In addition, he discerned a clear relationship between the amount of domains with problems in daily life and adjustment problems to incarceration. Empirical studies based on a stress-coping perspective that focused on juvenile inmates, showed individual differences in adjustment to detention. Individual differences in adjustment to detention have been found with regard to coping style (Eftekhari, Turner & Larimer, 2004;

Harvey, 2007; Ireland, 2001; Ireland, Boustead & Ireland, 2005), age (Gover, MacKenzie & Armstrong, 2000; Ireland, Boustead & Ireland, 2004), minority group (Adams, 1992; Gover et al., 2000; Klooster et al., 1999), and criminal history (Gover et al., 2000; Harvey, 2007; Mohino, Kirchner & Forms, 2004).

Coping styles

The literature about coping with incarceration observes that there are differences in the coping styles used by people to deal with these stressful situations. Some styles are adequate, while others are not. Adequate coping styles will ultimately result in minimal psychological distress, sufficient self-esteem, and few or no behavioural problems. In the literature, two adequate coping styles have been distinguished: a coping style in which someone deals with problems in a rational manner and looks for alternatives ('rational coping'), and a coping style in which someone distances himself from the stressful events in order to be able to deal with them in this way, thus minimising the impact of the emotions ('detached coping'). These are so-called 'problem-oriented' coping styles (Lazarus, 2000). Adequate coping styles are related to less psychological pain, sufficient self-esteem, and the absence of behavioural problems during incarceration (see e.g., Ireland, Boustead & Ireland, 2005).

Inadequate coping styles are characterised by, e.g., the feeling of being overwhelmed by stressful events and an emotional response if they continue ('emotional coping'), or by someone becoming distant from his social environment ('avoidance coping'). Although the latter coping style is effective in the short term, studies among the general inmate population show that 'avoidance coping' makes it more difficult to adjust to stressful situations (see Eftekhari, Turner & Larimer, 2004; Ireland et al., 2005). These coping styles appear to be used mainly in situations that are considered unalterable (see e.g. Harvey, 2007).

Among juvenile inmates, a clear association has been found between adequate coping styles and fewer psychological problems, whereas inadequate coping styles, by contrast, are accompanied by emotional problems like fear (Boustead & Ireland, 2005; Harvey, 2007; Ireland, 2007) or anger (Eftekhari et al., 2004). Boustead & Ireland (2005) have conducted a study in the UK among adolescent (aged 15-17) and young adult inmates (aged 18-21) into the association between coping styles and fear. Ireland and colleagues found that emotional coping is linked to more psychological problems (a combination of feelings of fear, depression, and insomnia), whereas rational coping strategies are connected to fewer psychological problems. Rational coping strategies therefore appear to be effective for young inmates as well. Eftekhari et al. (2004) studied the connection between anger, avoidance coping, and drug use in American adolescent male inmates (aged 15-20; the average age being 16.7). The researchers found a clear connection between avoidance coping styles and inwardly as well as outwardly directed anger (shouting, slamming doors).

Age

According to Adams (1992), several studies show that young people in custody commit offences and exhibit problem behaviour more frequently than adults do. We are not aware of any studies in which young people and adults have been compared with regard to the emotions they express during their custody. In two studies, however, juvenile inmates in different age groups have been compared (Gover et al., 2000; Ireland et al., 2004). Amongst other things, both studies focused on fear, but showed contradictory results.

Ireland, Boustead and Ireland (2004) studied the psychological problems amongst 108 British young adult inmates (aged 19-21) and adolescent inmates (aged 15-17). They found that psychological problems, including fear, are more frequently found in young adult inmates (aged 18-21) than in adolescents (aged 15-17). According to Ireland et al. (2004), these age differences relate to the development of coping styles during adolescence. Adolescents do have a limited series of coping strategies compared to young adults. Young adult inmates more often use emotional and avoidance coping strategies than adolescent inmates do. On the other hand, Gover et al. (2000) found a negative relation between the age and fear of juvenile inmates. They studied the relation of feelings of fear with individual characteristics (age, ethnic origin, previous convictions, type of offense, use of drugs, and violence in the family) and environmental characteristics (the level of control in the detention centre, safety, the fairness of procedures, and the staff-inmate ratio) amongst 3.986 juvenile inmates in the United States. Gover and colleagues found that the older the inmates, the lower the likelihood of fear. According to Gover et al. (2000), older inmates are more capable of dealing with a stressful situation than younger inmates.

In short, the literature shows mixed findings on the association of age with emotional reactions during incarceration.

Ethnic origin

In the Anglo-Saxon literature, differences were found between ethic origin groups in the way they adjust to incarceration and the associated emotions (Adams, 1992; Gover et al., 2000). Gover et al. (2000) found that Caucasian American boys reported higher levels of fear than juveniles from other origin groups. According to Adams (1992: 298), one explanation for the finding that Afro-Americans showed lower levels of fear than Caucasian Americans may be that black inmates in the US exhibit less cultural diversity, which allows for an ethnic solidarity that helps them cope with the tough life in prison. Adams also lists an alternative explanation, namely that many black inmates in the US come from a ghetto environment, where men are exposed from a young age to survival strategies that are useful to them in prison.

In the Netherlands, Klooster et al. (1999) have been the only ones to study the way in which boys from different ethnic minority groups experience their custody. They compared the experiences of Antillean, Surinamese, Moroccan, and Turkish boys. A number of differences were found between the different origin groups with regard to the emotions they experience. According to Klooster et al. (1999: 30) Antillean boys, for instance, will not easily show remorse publicly, but that does not mean they do not feel guilty. Moroccan boys will rather deny to have committed any offences, because they have no faith that the penal system will reward them for confessing to an offence. Among these young people, therefore, there is a more general mistrust in justice (see also Van Gemert, 1998). On the other hand, Klooster and colleagues (1999) also observed that Moroccan boys in particular benefit from the structure of juvenile detention. Turkish boys appear to be mainly ashamed of the fact they are being penalised. 'Serving their time' in detention does not increase the status of young people from this origin group, because their social network disapproves of their behaviour.

Criminal history

Studies among adult inmate populations in the US show differences in their coping with incarceration between first-time offenders, and those who have been previously incarcerated. However, the findings are not univocal. In his review study, Adams (1992) states that it is not clear to what extent previous experiences with incarceration affect the (emotional) adjustment to detention. With regard to young people, the association between previous experiences with incarceration and emotional reactions to custody is not clear either. In those studies in which differences are found, these findings relate mainly to different coping styles (Mohino et al., 2004).

Other studies do not find differences in emotional reactions to incarceration with regard to criminal history. In their study among nearly 4000 American teenage inmates, for instance, Gover et al. (2000) found no differences between first-time offenders and recidivists regarding the extent in which they experienced fear during their incarceration. Harvey (2007) compared British young adult first-time offenders (aged 18-21) and recidivists. However, in spite of their familiarity with the situation, recidivists were shown to experience emotional problems similar to first-time offenders. However, Harvey did observe differences in the type of stress experienced. First-time offenders appeared to struggle with feelings of uncertainty more often than recidivists did, whereas the stress among the recidivists was related mainly to feelings of loss of control and freedom.

3.2.2 *Characteristics of incarceration*

Studies based on the stress-coping perspective and the deprivation and importation model have provided insights into the association between environmental characteristics and adjustment to custody and, consequently, into the emotional responses experienced by the inmates. With regard to adult inmates, studies investigated a large number of environmental characteristics, such as the incarceration regime, or the physical environment of the incarceration. With regard to juveniles, research focused on the phase of the incarceration (Brown & Ireland, 2006; Harvey, 2007; Ireland et al., 2001; Ireland et al., 2006; Mohino et al., 2004), the activities during incarceration, the type of detention centre, and the (experienced) fairness of sanctions (Gover et al., 2000).

Phase of custody

An important finding is that the initial period of incarceration is experienced as very stressful. This phase is regarded as a high-risk period for self-harm, rule breaking and aggressive behaviour (Adams, 1992; Harvey, 2007), as well as for emotional problems, such as fear (Harvey, 2007; Brown & Ireland, 2006). Besides, a single study also showed that in the first phase of incarceration juveniles are experiencing higher levels of shame and guilt (Hosser et al., 2005; Hosser et al., 2008).

Harvey (2007) looked at the level of stress of young adult inmates three days after their arrival at a detention centre. He interviewed 70 men aged 18 to 21 in a British prison. The level of psychological stress suffered by these young men in this initial phase was high. The study shows that, in these first days in particular, the inmates a) were obsessed with their own safety; b) were uncertain about what would happen (the course of their criminal case); c) experienced feelings of loss of control and freedom; and d) experienced feelings of separation and loss of family members and friends. The loss of control and freedom are experiences that play a role especially during the first phase of the transition to the deprivation of liberty. Not only the reduction in control during the incarceration is experienced as being difficult, the reduction in control over what happened outside detention also proved difficult to accept. The separation from family members and other loved ones outside the prison proved to be a difficult aspect for the juveniles as well. During this initial phase of their incarceration, the young men refused to accept the reality of their custody and refused to bond with their new social environment. This increased their feelings of uncertainty and fear.

Coping strategies do change during the period juveniles are incarcerated (Mohino et al., 2004), just like the intensity of the associated emotions (Brown & Ireland, 2006; Hosser et al., 2005; Hosser et al., 2008). Mohino et al. (2004) studied the styles of coping among young male inmates and,

among other things, looked at a so-called emotional coping style. In a Spanish prison, 107 male inmates (aged 18-25) filled out a questionnaire that focused on coping styles. The time the young people had been incarcerated varied from a few days to a maximum of 53 months. This study found that juveniles who had been incarcerated for a short period of time used different coping strategies than those who had been incarcerated longer. Young men who had only been incarcerated for a short time (less than three months) were found to use the expression of negative emotions ('emotional discharge'; no further specification of the type of emotions) as a coping strategy for stressful situations more often, and did not look for constructive ways of dealing with stressful situations ('positive reappraisal') as often as young men who had been in the institution for a longer period of time.
Brown and Ireland (2006) found that juveniles change their type of coping strategy and the associated emotions during their stay in custody. Among 133 young British inmates, Brown and Ireland (2006) studied the connection between a change in coping style and changes in feelings of fear and depression. Juveniles were given a questionnaire shortly after their arrival at the detention centre and again six weeks later. During this period, Brown and Ireland observed a significant reduction in feelings of fear and depression. The respondents also reported changes in their coping styles during this 6-week period. Both a reduction in emotional coping and an increase in independent coping strategies were observed. Changes in coping styles were linked to changes in feelings of fear and depression. Taking into account different types of coping strategies, Brown and Ireland (2006) found that young people in whom a reduction in the emotional coping with the stressful situation was observed (fewer feelings of worthlessness and unimportance) also exhibited fewer feelings of fear and depression. The increased use of an independent coping style (taking little notice of the environment) also proved to be associated with a greater reduction in, for instance, feelings of fear.

Feelings of shame and guilt experienced by juvenile inmates also decrease as the duration of the incarceration increases. Hosser et al. (2005; see also Hosser et al., 2008) followed the development of feelings of guilt and shame during incarceration in a group of 447 male adolescent and young adult inmates (aged 14-24) from six detention centres in North Germany. The boys were interviewed three times: at the start of the incarceration, after three months, and shortly before they were released. This study shows that a significant proportion of the young men do not have feelings of shame and guilt but that, for the percentage of boys who do have these feelings, these feelings are highest at the start of custody. At the beginning, less than a third of the boys indicated they had felt guilty in the preceding 7 day, while almost two thirds of the boys indicated that they had not been ashamed of anything in the preceding 7 days. In the subsequent measurings, the percentage of boys who did not report to have had any feelings of shame or guilt increased, whereas the percentage of young people who regularly or frequently experienced feelings of guilt and shame decreased. The authors explain the low percentage of inmates who experience feelings of shame or guilt by pointing out possible neutralisation techniques that occur early in the incarceration. A possible explanation for the decrease in the percentage of young people reporting feelings of guilt and shame as the duration of the custody increases is the fact that young delinquents rapidly adjust to the culture in prison (prisonisation).

A process of adjustment in the initial period of custody
The duration of the custody goes hand-in-hand with changes in coping styles, and the longer the young people are incarcerated, the more they experience a reduction in stress and associated emotions. How does this process work? Harvey (2007) described this process in a study conducted among 28 young male British inmates (aged 18-21). These young men were interviewed 3, 10, and 30 days after their arrival. According to Harvey, three phases can be distinguished in the adjustment process of inmates: a) ‘liminality’, b) ‘acceptance’, and c) ‘equilibrium’. With the transition to each new phase, the level of adjustment to the incarceration environment increases and the negative emotional and psychological reactions of inmates decrease. With this study, Harvey shows that the adjustment to a custodial situation is a dynamic process. Yet, he did observe that inmates did not only progress from liminality to acceptance to equilibrium, but could also relapse to an earlier phase. This was the case, for instance, when they broke the rules or when they were transited to other units.

During the first phase, the ‘liminality’ phase, no adjustment at all was found to the new situation. This first phase in a custodial situation is very stressful. It is a phase of ‘self-reflection’ (see also Greve & Enzmann, 2003), in which emotions are experienced strongly. According to Harvey, these emotions are mainly feelings of fear, but guilt and shame are also emotions that were found to occur during this phase. The inmates felt themselves to be in-between two worlds, where they no longer had a ‘grip’ on their own life. In most inmates, this realisation was accompanied by shock and disbelief that they were actually in custody. Young people who got stuck in this phase were shown to find it difficult to regulate their emotions during the period of custody. To make the custody more bearable, the young people who got stuck in the first phase ‘blocked out’ the outside social world. This manifested itself, for instance, in a refusal to maintain contact with family members.
As the length of the period of incarceration progressed, the young inmates started to accept the situation in which they found themselves. This second phase, the ‘acceptance’ phase, was characterised by a sense of resignation to the situation, and by an increased bonding with the enforced

environment. The acceptance makes adjustment to the custody possible. There was evidence of social adjustment, both to fellow group members and to group leaders. Furthermore, the young people experienced the advantages of a structured regime and felt safer than at the beginning of their incarceration. Harvey also observed that ties with family members were continued or re-established. During this phase, the boys seemed to be more able of regulating their thoughts and feelings. According to Harvey (p. 68), this is a combination of emotion-oriented coping and problem-oriented coping (see also Lazarus, 2000). Both forms of coping were necessary and complemented each other, so as to enable the young people to deal with the new situation in an effective manner. According to Harvey, those who dealt well with the emotional stress they were experiencing were also in better control of their social and practical life in prison.
A small proportion of the young men interviewed in the study by Harvey (2007) achieved the 'equilibrium' phase in the first month of custody. According to Harvey, this third phase is characterised by the continued acceptance of the reality of the situation, and an increase in self-esteem. The inmates began to experience more positive emotions. In addition to the absence of negative emotions, these young men also had a more positive outlook in terms of dealing with the difficulties of the deprivation of liberty, and proved to be more optimistic than before. They also proved to be more able to regulate their thoughts and emotions. Regulation and a stabilisation of thoughts and emotions proved to be an essential element for psychological survival in a new situation (Harvey, 2007: 71). During this phase, inmates know how to deal with stress during incarceration. Being able to keep psychological stress under control proved to be less difficult for the young people. They became more skilful at dealing with new stressful experiences in the group. They had discovered effective coping strategies for themselves (both problem-oriented and emotion-oriented coping strategies) to deal with the difficulties of the deprivation of liberty. According to Harvey (p. 72), it is very important that young inmates achieve this phase, since it means that they experience less stress and exhibit fewer emotional problems.

Factors that make the transition to a subsequent adjustment phase more difficult were:
- kicking a drug habit (p. 60): drug users who are trying to kick the habit are shown to stay in the first phase longer than non-drug users. In other words, drug use delays the adjustment to a custodial situation;
- being moved to different departments (p. 61): Harvey's study shows that a move to other units causes some male inmates to keep experiencing feelings of unsafety; they remain fearful. These young people have to start adjusting to the situation all over again.

Activities, type of institution and sanctions
We found one study that focused on the association between emotional reactions of juveniles and other characteristics of incarceration, like activities, type of institution, and sanctions (Gover et al., 2000). Gover et al. (2000) studied the relation of a variety of characteristics of a detention centre with the levels of fear of 3,986 young male inmates (mean age 16), distributed among 48 juvenile detention centres in the US. Taking into account various individual characteristics and environmental characteristics, they found that in institutions where inmates participate in structured activities to a greater extent, the boys reported fewer feelings of fear. Furthermore, Gover et al. (2000) also found a connection between the level of fear of juveniles and the type of institution. In a multi-level analysis, they assessed to what extent the type of institution explains the differences in the levels of fear among young people. They made a distinction between traditional juvenile detention centres (22) and so-called 'boot camps' (26). Taking into account the various individual and institutional background characteristics, they found that boys incarcerated in boot camps experienced stronger feelings of fear than boys in other centres did.
Finally, Gover et al. also found an association between the perceived fairness of punishments/sanctions during the incarceration and fear levels of juveniles. Taking into account various other characteristics of the incarceration regime and the background characteristics of the young people themselves, they found that the extent to which young people considered the disciplinary procedures as unfair is related to stronger feelings of fear (see also Harvey, 2007; Liebling, 2006).

3.2.3 Social support

Someone's social environment is an important factor for the way in which he or she deals with a new experience. In general, people will experience the transition to a new situation as less stressful if they receive sufficient social support (Biggam & Power, 1997; Maitland & Sluder, 1996; Underwood, 2000).[5] What can we say about this with regard to juveniles who have been incarcerated? We found little support on this topic that applied to juvenile inmates. The studies on social support in which juvenile inmates were the subject showed that the concept of social support is a complex one that has been operationalised in different ways. Some studies define social support as the verbal support of significant others (Biggam & Power, 1997), while other define it as the accepted trust

5 Studies among general populations show that social support can reduce the painful consequences of a stressful experience (for instance: less fear, helplessness) or can result in improved overall well-being. It has also been found that social support acts as a moderator or buffer, because social support makes someone more able to resist different stressful experiences. However, the majority of these studies relate to research into the way people handle psychological or physical problem situations.

and received respect of staff members (Harvey, 2007), or the social norms of the peer group (Harvey, 2007).These different operationalisations of the concept of social support make it difficult to draw conclusions about the relation between support of the social environment and emotional reactions to incarceration.

Inmates may receive social support from, for instance, family members (parents, brothers/sisters) or friends: the external social environment. Support from the external social environment can be an important factor that might contribute to a young person's ability to cope with a stressful experience like incarceration, and that can reduce the painful consequences of the custody (Biggam & Power, 1997; Harvey, 2007). However, the studies among juvenile inmates we found on this subject did not show a clear relation between external social support and emotional responses of juveniles, such as reduced fear (Biggam & Power, 1997). Biggam and Power (1997) studied the experienced social support outside the prison in relation to the experiencing of psychological distress (fear, depression, hopelessness) among 125 young male inmates (aged 16-21) in Scotland. The boys had been incarcerated for an average of 17.3 months. The majority of boys received external social support from one of their parents, a brother or sister, or a (girl)friend, but Biggam and Power did not find a clear correlation between experienced external social support and a reduction in fear.

We found some evidence for a relation between perceived internal social support from staff members and emotional responses of juveniles (Biggam & Power, 1997; Harvey, 2007).[6] In the previously described study among juveniles in Scotland, Biggam and Power (1997) found that a lack of internal social support from staff members is positively associated with higher levels of fear. According to Biggam and Power, internal social support is helpful in managing a stressful situation (it functions as 'coping assistance'). Such support is mainly relevant for young perpetrators in institutions, as it is often their first time in custody, which means they have to deal with the loss of contact with family and friends that is a result of the incarceration.

6 Experienced social support is a complex phenomenon that is realised in the daily interaction between group workers and inmates. In a qualitative study among young inmates, Harvey (2007) meticulously describes how such support can be given shape. According to Harvey (2007: 79), it is mainly the inmate's perception of received social support that is relevant, and to a lesser extent the actual social support. What is important in the perception of received social support, are perceptions of safety, trust, and respect. Whether or not the young people experienced trust proved to be dependent on the way in which the group workers dealt with them on a daily basis. The young people trusted group workers if the group workers kept their promises and if the juveniles were able to tell the group leaders something in confidence without having to worry that other inmates or staff members would hear their complaints. A single study among adult inmates also shows that the way inmates feel they are treated by staff members is related to their psychological well-being (Liebling, 2006). Inmates who feel they are treated unfairly by staff members experience more psychological problems, like fear and depression, than inmates who feel that they are treated fairly by staff members.

The social contact between the inmates themselves also affects the adjustment to custody and the emotions that are experienced and demonstrated. Referring to Sykes (1958), Harvey (2007) asserts that the interaction with group members and entering into social relations with these group members is important for the adjustment to the custody situation. In his study among young British inmates, Harvey (2007) found that the 'inmate code' is mainly functional for reducing the stress of custody for those who are by nature more assertive and use effective coping strategies. For juveniles who suffer more acute psychological stress and who exhibit their weakness and vulnerability, the 'inmate code' proved to be dysfunctional. According to Harvey (2007), those young people who needed the support the most were often afraid to seek help from the staff, as they were worried about the vulnerability this might reveal to their fellow group members.

3.3 Emotions during incarceration and recidivism

The fourth question in this study is whether the literature contains indications that emotions experienced during incarceration affect recidivism. In literature that specifically relates to juveniles, hardly any indication can be found to support this premise (the exception is Hosser et al., 2005). The majority of studies aimed at recidivism focus on the effects that interventions have on recidivism. Studies into emotions during custody in relation to recidivism are rare, but have recently been initiated (Tangney et al., 2007a). In the context of the moral development of juveniles, there is an interest in this subject matter in the Netherlands as well (see, for instance, Le Sage et al., 2006). Some studies have focused on the predictive value of anger (Loza & Loza-Fanous, 1999), shame, or guilt (Tangney et al., 2007a). These studies focus on emotions as a characteristic of the personality of inmates: the dispositional emotions (see Chapter 1). Research on the predictive value of dispositional emotions observed during custody for recidivism is still in its infancy and is mainly guided by psychological studies about moral emotions.

In psychological research, there is a perspective that focuses on the functioning and development of moral emotions and the effects of these emotions on (offending) behaviour. Emotions are regarded as the key to the motivational system (Stegge, 2006; Tangney, 2007). Shame, guilt, and pride act as emotional barometers that give immediate and noticeable feedback about what someone considers to be morally and socially acceptable. This feedback stops someone from exhibiting similar behaviour again or, conversely, encourages similar behaviour. When we break rules or make a mistake, negative feelings of shame or guilt are generated to stop us from making the same mistake in future. If we do something well, feelings of pride may be generated which stimulate us to exhibit similar behaviour again (Tangney et al., 2007b: 347). With regard to serious juvenile delinquents, it has been observed, for instance, that feelings of guilt, shame, and empathy are underdeveloped (see Le Sage, 2006).

In the criminological and psychological literature, different (moral) emotions observed during incarceration have been associated with recidivism of juvenile delinquents. These emotions are anger (Loza & Loza-Fanous, 1999), shame (Ferwerda et al., 2006; Hosser et al., 2005; Hosser et al., 2008; see also Tibbetts, 2003), guilt (Hosser et al., 2005; Hosser et al., 2008; Tibbetts, 2003), and pride (Hudley, 1992; Tibbetts, 2003).[7] As mentioned before, research is still in its infancy and we can not draw firm conclusions on the findings concerning the predictive value of emotional responses during incarceration on recidivism.

Anger

Anger, or its more intense variant rage, is a negatively charged emotion that is experienced subjectively as a hostile reaction, aimed at someone or something who/that is regarded as the source of the anger. Someone who is angry feels that something or someone else has hostile intentions toward him and wants to harm him. These provocations can take the form of an insult, a treatment that is experienced as unfair or dishonest, or intentional opposition (Novaco, 2000). Anger is experienced as a deserved response to injustice (Haidt, 2003: 856). Anger has an important function for people when it comes to survival and being able to sustain oneself in, for instance, a social context (Novaco, 2000). People who are angry also feel motivated to take revenge on whatever or whomever causes their anger or rage (or on a substitute for these persons or institutions), which does not mean that they will actually do so in each situation (Haidt, 2003: 856).

Although feelings of anger may be functional, the emotion has a number of adverse effects that will restrict someone's functioning. For instance, someone will no longer be able to process information in a normal manner. Anger also limits someone's cognitive control of the situation. Anger may encourage aggressive behaviour, resulting in someone suffering damage or injury. In turn, this damage or injury may have undesirable repercussions for the angry person. Research also shows that people who are angry are not optimally alert, cautious, empathic, careful, or physically healthy (Novaco, 2000).

7 Empathy, or rather the lack of empathy, has also been associated with antisocial behaviour, but looking at this aspect in more detail falls outside the scope of this study.

Although research has shown a relation between anger and aggression, empirical studies do not show a univocal picture of the predictive value of anger on misconduct during custody, or on recidivism after incarceration (Loza & Loza-Fanous, 1999; Mills & Kroner, 2003). A review study by Loza and Loza-Fanous (1999) shows, for instance, that support has been found for the relationship between anger and aggressive behaviour, both in laboratory studies, and in studies among juvenile and adult inmates. However, anger is mainly regarded as a mediating factor for aggressive behaviour, and a motivator for criminal behaviour and recidivism, or personal attributes (disposition) that make someone more likely to reoffend. Juveniles with behavioural problems, in particular, exhibit more anger and are less able to regulate their anger than young people who do not have behavioural problems. These are mainly young people who regularly experience feelings of anger, dispositional anger, and who attribute the cause of their anger to the hostile intentions of others (see Stegge, 2006: 37-38 for references).

Experiencing only anger during incarceration has little predictive value for recidivism after incarceration (Loza & Loza-Fanous, 1999; see also Mills & Kroner, 2003), as anger alone need not necessarily lead to aggression (Loza & Loza-Fanous, 1999) and aggression is mostly caused by a cumulation of (social and biological) factors. Conversely, aggressive behaviour, either driven by instinctive or instrumental emotion, is not always related to anger. Furthermore, in many situations, aggressive behaviour does not constitute an offence. In conclusion, studies show that violent offences also take place without anger being a factor. In the case of inmates, as well, a relationship cannot always be found between anger and violent behaviour during incarceration (for more details, see the review study by Loza and Loza-Fanous, 1999).

Shame

Feelings of shame may be experienced, for instance when someone has exhibited behaviour that conflicts with his or her moral views (Lewis, 2000). According to Tibbetts (2003), in the criminological literature, shame is often confused with guilt, whereas psychological research shows that there are clear differences in the way these feelings are experienced (see also Tangney, 2000b; Tangney et al. 2007b; Tibbetts, 2003). When experiencing shame, someone feels that he has personally failed and fallen short of his own moral standards. That person will feel degraded and inferior, and his or her self-respect is affected. Feelings of shame are accompanied by painful feelings of being worthless or powerless as a result of a devaluation of the self-image (Tangney, 2000b; Tangney et al., 2007b; Tibbets, 2003). Someone who is ashamed considers *himself* to be a bad person. Feelings of shame are associated with a desire to be able to curl up in a corner, to hide or to flee. According to the psychological literature, feelings of shame, because of their comprehensive character, are generally experienced as more painful than other moral emotions, like guilt (see Tangney, 1998). Feelings of shame make someone worry about how others see him or her, although this does not necessarily mean that these others need in fact be present. From this perspective, feelings of shame may be experienced because someone has committed an offence or continues to do so, but also because someone is subjected to judicial custody and worries what others think about this.

We found one Dutch study that has examined the relationship between the experiencing of shame and recidivism (Ferwerda et al., 2006). Ferwerda and colleagues (2006) studied this relationship among young people who had been given a Halt (*community service*) sanction. Their study shows that at T1 young people who reported that they were ashamed of their offence reported fewer subsequent offences at T2, even when allowances are made for different background characteristics. However, the sample consists of juveniles who have committed a minor offence followed by a light sanction, and it remains to be seen whether the shame experienced by juveniles in custody is also linked to a reduction in delinquency levels.

Research into the effects of shame experienced by juvenile inmates on the level of recidivism has not yet been able to provide clarity regarding this relationship. The only study among juvenile inmates that we are aware of, in which the relationship between shame and recidivism is studied, is the aforementioned study by Hosser et al. (2005; Hosser et al., 2008) among German male adolescents and young adults. Taking into account different individual and family risk factors for delinquency, they did not find that self-reported feelings of shame at the start of the custody had any significant effects on recidivism after the incarceration. In addition, Hosser et al. did not find any effect of shame on recidivism among subgroups of delinquents.

In the criminological literature, the relationship between feelings of shame and recidivism has only been studied to a limited extent (see Tibbetts, 2003 for an overview). The research suggests that there is a negative connection between feelings of shame and delinquency. In psychological research, shame in relation to antisocial behaviour is studied more closely. Contrary to the findings from criminological studies, psychological studies find a positive relationship between (mainly dispositional) shame and antisocial behaviour (see, for instance, Tangney et al., 1995; Tangney et al., 2007b). According to Tibbetts (2003: 105), criminological studies are based on (outdated) traditional definitions of shame and ignore the more accurate description that is used in psychology (Tangney, 2000b; Tangney et al., 2007b). In criminological research, shame is a container concept without making a clear distinction between shame, guilt, and embarrassment (Tangney, 2007b; Gilbert, 1998). That this distinction is relevant with regard to delinquency and recidivism has been shown in psychological research (see e.g. Hosser et al., 2003; 2008; Tangney et al., 2007; Tibbetts, 2003).

Guilt

Contrary to shame, where a person feels bad about himself, people who suffer from guilt feel bad about specific behaviour they have exhibited, or have failed to exhibit. Whereas in the case of shame the focus is mainly on the 'self', in the cognitive evaluation that is associated with feelings of guilt, a person focuses on his or her (rule-breaking) behaviour and not on him/herself (Tangney, 1995; Tangney, 2007b). People who feel guilty report that, in their thoughts, they repeatedly examine the rule-breaking behaviour and wonder why they acted the way they did, and why they did not act differently. Feelings of guilt are less painful and threatening than feelings of shame because the primary focus is on specific behaviour and not on the individual. Feelings of guilt motivate a person into a positive direction towards change or rehabilitation (Baumeister, Stillwell & Heaherton, 1995; in Dearing et al., 2005: 1393). Feelings of guilt are characterised by a person experiencing stress about what he or she did wrong. Guilt encourages restorative behaviour: confessing, apologising, or remedying the mistake in some way (Tangney, 1995; Tangney et al., 2007). It may be expected that feelings of guilt are related to the commission of fewer offences and a reduction in recidivism (Tangney et al., 2007a; Weijers, 2000). Research in Australia and New Zealand into the effects of restorative justice conferences on recidivism shows, that a factor like 'remorse', when exhibited during a restorative justice conference, is an important predictor for reduced recidivism (Daly, 2005; Morris & Maxwell, 2005). However, this does not mean that invoking such moral feelings does actually result in reduced recidivism (Daly, 2005). And with regard to custody, there are many more relevant factors that play a role, such as the family members or family context, or the group of friends the young person becomes (re)involved with after the custody. It is feasible that, in this context, the reactions of family members to the offence and the custody will set in motion a process that can aid the young person in remaining 'on the straight and narrow' in the future. Despite this complexity and lack of clarity, the studies still show a connection between feelings of guilt and reduced recidivism.

Lately, the relationship between guilt and recidivism has been the subject of more recent empirical criminological studies (Hosser et al., 2003; Hosser et al., 2008; Tangney et al. 2007a; Tibbetts, 2003). With regard to juveniles in custody, we found one study that investigated this relationship (Hosser et al., 2005; see also Hosser et al., 2008). Hosser and colleagues (2005) studied young male inmates to determine to what extent feelings of guilt during incarceration are connected to recidivism in the first 24 months after incarceration. They did not find a direct (statistically significant) effect of guilt on recidivism, but they did find a negative trend (more feelings of guilt, declining recidivism, yet no significant effect). Besides, they did find effects of an interaction between the offence for which the young people were incarcerated and feelings of guilt in relation to subsequent recidivism. Young people who were incarcerated because of violent offences against others, and who experienced feelings of guilt during custody, were less inclined to recidivism (a lower hazard ratio) than young people who were incarcerated because of violent offences, but who did not appear to feel guilt.

Pride

Pride may be described as a feeling where 'a person feels responsible for achieving a socially desirable objective or for being a socially appreciated person' (Mascolo & Fischer, 1995: 65). Pride reinforces someone's self-esteem and guides behaviour that conforms to the social values of the group someone is associated with. Experiencing pride is clearly related to subcultural values. Someone may feel pride because he has done something that is appreciated in his subculture and causes others to look up to him. Pride is dependent on the perceived response of peers, or fellow group members,

Tibbetts (2003) examined the relationship between pride and delinquency. According to Tibbetts, pride in relation to delinquent behaviour has hardly been the subject of any studies. Little is therefore known about the predictive value of this emotion when it comes to committing offences, and equally little is known about the differences in the levels of pride between delinquent and non-delinquent young people. One study looks at the perceived causes of pride among delinquent juveniles (Hudley, 1992). Hudley (1992) studied differences between young people in a custodial institution and young people at a high school in the US, with respect to the causes of pride as described by the young people themselves. Young inmates were more likely to ascribe the causes of feelings of pride to individual characteristics (for instance physical strength) than the students. Young inmates did not describe the commission of offences as one of the reasons for feelings of pride. Referring to a study by Simour (1997), Tibbets (2003) asserts that indications were found that pride is associated with attitudes and behaviour that are positive with respect to the commission of offences. However, Tibbetts (2003) also feels that quite a few question marks remain about the way in which pride is operationalised in the study concerned.

3.4 Conclusion

Incarceration can be emotionally stressful. An adequate adjustment to incarceration results in fewer behavioural problems and physical and psychological problems among young inmates. An inadequate adjustment to custody is associated with, for instance, strong emotions of fear or anger, which may be expressed in problem behaviour. Thus, an adequate adjustment to custody is important to both staff and juvenile inmates. Van Binsbergen (2003) used a model of Diclemente and Pochanski to investigate the motivation of Dutch juveniles for a treatment programme. She found that negative emotions during imprisonment are associated with defiance and can reduce the potential behavioural change (next to other individual and social risk factors). However, it was not the purpose of this study to investigate the motivation for behavioural change.

In this chapter, we first studied literature concerning the relations between individual, environmental, and social characteristics on the one hand, and emotional responses of juvenile inmates on the other. Empirical research mainly focused only indirectly on this relation. The majority of studies relate to Anglo-Saxon study groups, more specifically British and American juvenile inmates. An occasional study takes young inmates in Germany or Spain as its subject. We found one Dutch study that discusses the relation between custody and the emotions of incarcerated young people.

Emotions and incarceration
According to the literature, the following individual characteristics of juvenile inmates are associated to emotions during incarceration:
- the occurrence of multiple problems is associated with high levels of emotional stress;
- problem-oriented coping styles are accompanied by lower levels of emotional stress than emotion-oriented coping styles. These latter strategies are accompanied by higher levels of fear;
- ethnic origin groups differ in their emotional reactions to being incarcerated;
- the associations of age and a criminal history with emotional stress during incarceration are not clear for juveniles.

Empirical studies found that specific characteristics of incarceration are associated with (strong) emotional stress in juveniles and that these may inhibit an adequate adjustment to incarceration. These are the following characteristics:
- the phase of incarceration. During the initial phase of incarceration, higher levels of emotional stress (fear, guilt, shame) are experienced than later on;

- the availability and the inmate's use of structured activities (school, leisure activities, sports) is associated with lower levels of emotional stress (fear).

We also searched for a relation between aspects of the juvenile's social environment and emotional stress. Empirical research has focused on social support. This seems, however, to be a complex construct. The findings in the literature do not allow for univocal conclusions, but we found indications that internal social support by staff members may reduce emotional stress in juvenile inmates.

Emotions and recidivism

Secondly, we studied the relation between emotional stress during incarceration and recidivism. The few studies on this topic focused on moral emotions like anger, shame, guilt, and pride. In the theory, it is assumed that anger, shame, and pride do not inhibit crime and may even stimulate crime, while guilt does have an inhibiting effect on crime. The empirical research has hardly examined these relations. The studies on this topic showed that:

- anger during custody is shown to be associated to misconduct during incarceration or recidivism in some studies, but according to a review study, this relationship was not evident in other studies. Anger alone need not result in misconduct or recidivism. There is, therefore, no univocal view concerning the connection between anger and recidivism;
- no direct association is found of shame experienced by juvenile inmates with recidivism;
- among juvenile inmates, no direct connection was found between guilt felt during incarceration and recidivism. However, one German study shows that violent offenders who felt guilty about their offence during custody committed fewer offences after their release than violent offenders who did not experience feelings of guilt. These findings are hopeful, but more research is needed, since it is not clear to what extent the effects of feelings of guilt are unique to recidivism when taking into account (social and individual) background characteristics;
- pride during custody in relation to recidivism was not studied.

Study 2: Interviews with experts

4 Individual characteristics

The second part of this study reports on interviews with experts from Dutch correctional institutions for juvenile offenders regarding their experiences with different emotional reactions of the young detainees. We interviewed a total of 21 experts (both group leaders and behavioural scientists) from four correctional institutions for juvenile offenders. In semi-structured interviews, six emotions were put before the experts with the question whether or not they recognised these emotions in young people in custodial centres. Another question was whether or not, according to the experts, these emotions were related to characteristics of the custody, characteristics of the social environment, or individual characteristics. The emotions put before the experts were anger, shame, guilt, remorse, pride, and fear.
In this chapter, we will first describe how these emotions are expressed according to the experts and we will look at individual differences between juvenile inmates in their expression of these emotions. The next two chapters will describe the association of emotional reactions of juveniles with characteristics of the incarceration (Chapter 5) and the social environment (Chapter 6).

4.1 The emotions according to the experts

The findings of this study are based on the observations of group leaders and behavioural scientists (the experts), respectively. In this paragraph, we will describe whether, and if so, how often and in what manner, the different emotions have been identified in the young people through the observations of the experts.

Anger
The majority of experts observe anger in young people in custodial institutions. Eleven experts claim they observe anger often, while eight experts are not clear as to how often this emotion is observed. Only two experts claim that anger is observed only rarely.
According to the experts, anger can be expressed in different ways. These expressions may be non-verbal, verbal, or physical. The non-verbal expressions mentioned are gestures, facial expressions, and distancing oneself from the group. The experts often mention verbal expressions in particular. The specific expressions the experts mention most are cursing (13 of the 21), shouting (3 of the 21), and a generally rebellious attitude (3 of the 21). Physical expressions are observed by twelve experts, but to a much lesser extent than the non-verbal and verbal expressions. Physical expressions vary from kicking or hitting doors or walls and throwing projectiles to actual fighting.

Shame

The majority of experts say that shame in relation to the offence is observed only very occasionally (17 of the 21). Only one expert feels that shame in relation to the offence is seen regularly, while three experts have never observed feelings of shame in relation to the offence. Eight experts have observed that the emotion of shame in relation to the offence was expressed through the boys' unwillingness to discuss the offence, or because they reverted to lying about the committed offence. Nine experts also say that feelings of shame in relation to the offence are expressed during individual discussions, in which young people indicate that they are ashamed (7 of the 9). An occasional expert also mentions a behavioural expression, such as withdrawn behaviour (2 of the 9).

Most experts also observe feelings of shame in relation to being in custody rarely. Only three experts indicate that this emotion does not occur. Incidentally, there is no consensus about the extent to which such emotions occur. Nine experts have observed shame about being in custody in several boys, whereas seven experts feel that only some boys exhibit this emotion. These feelings have been observed based on occurrences, such as inmates lying to the external environment (mainly to their parents) about the their involvement in the offence (6 of the 16), inmates wanting to stop contact with their parents (2 of the 16), and based on personal discussions in which the boys have mentioned feeling ashamed with respect to their parents (3 of the 16).

Guilt

According to most of the group leaders, feelings of guilt do occur in young people in custodial institutions, but this emotion is not observed often. The make a distinction between feelings of guilt in relation to the offence and feelings of guilt in relation to being in custody. Feelings of guilt in relation to the offence are observed, but to a very limited extent. A considerable proportion of the experts (11 of the 21) assert that only the occasional boy exhibits genuine feelings of guilt in relation to the victim. A few experts feel that they observe such emotions somewhat more frequently (3 of the 21), or are not clear about the extent to which these feelings occur (6 of the 21). The experts say they do not often observe feelings of guilt in relation to the committed offence because these feelings rarely occur. According to three experts, showing feelings of guilt is regarded as a sign of weakness by fellow group members. The experts also say that showing guilt has both positive and negative consequences for the boys' criminal case. For this reason, some boys will never admit to guilt, whereas for others acknowledging guilt can actually result in a reduced sentence.

The twenty experts who have observed genuine guilt in relation to the offence (or victim) did so mainly on the basis of personal discussions with the young people (11 of the 20). They referred to the way in which the boys

would discuss the victim during these discussions and the remorse the experts observed in the boys. The experts also mentioned the boys' willingness to talk about the issue with the group leaders (3 of the 20), and the wish to be able to talk to the victim (4 of the 20).
Nineteen of the 21 experts occasionally observed feelings of guilt in relation to being in custody. There is no consensus about the extent to which this emotion occurs. Some experts say that many boys exhibit this emotion (7 of the 19) whereas others claim that it occurs never, or only to a very limited extent (4 of the 21). In eight cases, the extent to which the emotion occurs was not stated clearly. In an overwhelming majority of the cases, the experts refer to feelings of guilt in relation to the parents.

Pride
The experts observe feelings of pride in the boys. When it comes to this emotion, the distinction between feelings of pride in relation to the offence and feelings of pride in relation to the incarceration is also relevant. The extent to which expressions of feelings of pride in relation to the offence are observed is not always sufficiently clear. Only two experts claimed that these expressions of pride do not occur, while two experts indicated that these feelings occur in some cases, and four experts indicated that feelings of pride related to the committed offence occur regularly or frequently. The other experts (12 of the 21) only indicated that these expressions do occur.
The expressions that were mentioned as forming the basis on which the experts deduce the feelings of pride in relation to the offence are very univocal. All the experts referred to the boys bragging about the offence. This includes boasting about the offence, glorifying the offence, and comprehensively describing (all the aspects of) the offence. Three experts expressly referred to the possible presence of 'feigned pride'. They feel that, in some cases, the boys adopt an attitude rather than exhibit real pride in relation to the offence.

According to twelve experts, feelings of pride in relation to the incarceration do occur, but not as often as feelings of pride in relation to the offence. Two experts observe these feelings regularly; six experts observe these feelings in some individuals, while the extent to which the other experts observe these feelings is not clear. The expressions the experts interpret as pride in relation to being in custody nearly all consist of acting tough and bragging to fellow group members (11 of the 12). In some cases, the expression of pride consists of comments relating to an increase in status among the group of friends outside the institution, and in other cases it manifests itself in bragging about previous incarcerations (4 of the 12).
Six experts even claim that feelings of pride in relation to the incarceration never occur, at least not within the institution. Two of these six

experts do mention the possibility of feelings of pride being expressed in relation to individuals outside the institution.

Fear
Fear is an emotion that nearly all experts observe often in young people in custodial institutions. Only one expert claimed that he has not often come across this emotion. All experts observed that, especially at the start of the incarceration period, expressions of feelings of fear are a frequent occurrence. The experts recognise feelings of fear through a range of expressions. The expressions mentioned most often are: timid behaviour (10 of the 20), boys actually telling the group leaders that they are frightened (4 of the 20), and being more affectionate toward the group leaders (4 of the 20).

Remorse
Remorse is an emotion that the experts do not observe, or hardly ever observe, in the young people in custodial institutions. Nine experts referred to an occasional incidence, or called the extent to which this emotion occurs sporadic. Nine experts claimed that the emotion never occurs. In two cases, it is not clear to what extent the experts felt the emotion occurs. The experts who did refer to certain incidences list varying expressions that they have interpreted as indicating remorse. Grouped together, these expressions are: boys having trouble living with the fact of the offence; this translates into, for instance, sadness and having trouble sleeping (5 of the 11) as well as boys actively trying to improve their life; this translates into, for instance, the boy wanting to contact the victim at his own initiative, and improved behaviour within the group (5 of the 11).

Since remorse was observed so seldom by the experts, we were unable to analyse the relation between this emotional reaction and different aspects of the custody, the social environment, or individual characteristics of the juveniles. For this reason, we dropped 'remorse'.

4.2 Individual characteristics: age, ethnic group, and criminal history

4.2.1 Age

In the literature, contradictory results are found in relation to the emotions of juveniles during custody (Gover et al., 2000; Ireland et al., 2005). The experts were asked to what extent they observed age differences in the emotions. In most of the custodial institutions where the experts were engaged, boys of different ages were brought together in one residential group. In one custodial institution, boys under 16 were separated from boys who were 16 or older. In another custodial institution, the boys were accommodated on the basis of their destination in the institution (a group for intake, one for special care, et cetera).

Anger
Five experts either did not mention a possible relation between age and anger, or did not observe such an association.
The other eleven experts, however, *do* observe a link. According to seven of these experts, young boys react angrily to their custody more often than older boys. Young boys get angry more often because of their lack of understanding of their custody; because they do not understand how they got in this situation; or because they are more impulsive. Three other group leaders, by contrast, reported that it is especially the older boys who respond with anger or rage more often. The experts asserted that older boys have more difficulty accepting their punishment; have been in contact with the police more often and therefore react more angrily; or that older boys want to exhibit macho behaviour to their fellow group members more often, and therefore react more angrily.

Shame
Eleven experts did not mention an association between shame and age, and four experts felt that there is no such connection. Six experts do observe age differences in the feelings of shame in young inmates, but they gave little explanation for this opinion. According to three experts, young boys are more ashamed of the offence. Whether this also means that older boys do not experience this shame is not clear, because the observation of age differences in the experiencing of feelings of shame is also related to the openness of the young people.

Guilt
If the experts *did* observe feelings of guilt in the young people, they indicated that older boys feel guilty about the committed offence (four experts), whereas young boys feel guilty about being incarcerated in a correctional institution for juvenile offenders (four experts). Older boys supposedly feel guilty about the offence more often because they are more capable of thinking about their mistakes (and particularly the consequences of their mistake for their future), or because their conscience is better developed. Young boys are supposedly more likely to feel guilty about the incarceration because of what it does to their parents: they have not met the expectations of the parents and feel bad about what they have done to them, as one group leader explains:

> *'(...) Young boys do feel guilty, especially if the parents show their emotions, grief included. The boys feel like: it is because of me that they feel this way and I don't want my parents to be sad. (...) The young boys really want this very badly, because it means they can spend a little longer*

with mommy and daddy. They want to call home often and say: I feel so bad about what I have done to my parents and my parents are afraid to tell anyone at school that I am here now.' (GL 11)

Pride
Four experts also observe differences in age with regard to expressions of feelings of pride. Particularly boys who are older exhibit pride about the committed offence more often than young boys, these experts say.

Fear
Nine experts saw clear age differences in the level of fear among the young inmates. These experts are of the opinion that young boys are fearful more often than older boys are. The main reason they mentioned is that young boys are physically smaller than the older boys they are confronted with in the group, which feels threatening to the young boys (6 experts). One of these group leaders did, however, also comment that this type of fear is often short-lived, because the older boys are happy to take the young boys under their wing.
The fact that young boys exhibit fearful behaviour more often does not mean that older boys are not fearful, but the group workers particularly associated this fear with the phase of the custody the young people are in (see paragraph 5.2). Older boys, too, are fearful when they first enter the institution.

4.2.2 Ethnic groups

There are differences between boys from different ethnic origin groups with respect to the emotions they experience during custody (Adams, 1992; Klooster et al., 1999). With regard to feelings of fear, the international literature reports that Caucasian inmates are fearful more often than inmates from other origin groups (see, for instance, Adams, 1992). In the Netherlands, Klooster et al. (1999) have also found origin-related differences with regard to feelings of guilt and shame. Apparently, boys of Antillean and Moroccan ethnic origin exhibit hardly any feelings of guilt in relation to the committed offence, while boys from Turkish families are ashamed especially toward their family because they are incarcerated. What differences in the expression of emotions do the experts from the correctional institutions for juvenile offenders observe between ethnic origin groups?

Anger
Nine experts observed anger in boys from ethnic minorities more often than in native Dutch boys. According to these experts, boys of Antillean or Moroccan origin, in particular, appear to react angrily more often than boys from other ethnic minorities. One reason for this, the experts

mentioned, is that boys of these minority groups are abandoned by their parents as soon as they are incarcerated or, if the parents do visit, they make it very clear that the boy has disgraced the family honour. The fact that a boy has disappointed his parents and the consequence of the parents no longer coming to see the boy can result in very strong emotions, according to a group leader. Another expert thought that boys of ethnic minority groups feel they are less easily understood than boys of native Dutch origin are. Another reason that was mentioned, more specifically with regard to boys of Moroccan origin, is that their anger is the result of what they perceive to be unjust treatment. This perception is generated, for instance, by the fact that they are being dealt with by female group leaders, or because these boys feel that they are being slighted by the judicial authorities and society in general.

Shame

Boys who feel shame because of the offence they have committed are rare, said most of the experts. If the experts *do* observe examples of shame, this is mainly in connection with specific types of offences, such as sex offences (see below). When the experts do observe evidence of shame, they find that boys from ethnic minorities are less ashamed in relation to their offence than native Dutch boys, according to four experts.

Eleven experts do observe differences between ethnic origin groups when it comes to shame in relation to the incarceration. They particularly referred to boys with a Muslim background; these boys appear to be more ashamed of their incarceration than native Dutch boys. The main reason these experts gave for their observation is that, as a result of the fact that they are incarcerated, boys from ethnic minorities experience the disgrace of their environment more strongly through the reactions of their family members. Parents make it clear to the boy that he has discredited the family honour.

Guilt

Ten experts observed differences in the expression of guilt based on ethnic origin. Seven of these nine experts were of the opinion that native Dutch boys exhibit more feelings of guilt, whereas another expert, by contrast, felt that boys from ethnic minorities exhibit more feelings of guilt.

> *'To be honest, I do observe feelings of guilt relatively often amongst Dutch boys. You often see that those boys have feelings of guilt with regard to victims, and that they come from a family with strong bonds. Within their family, they received clear norms and values. Those boys are really educated by their parents. You never see* [feelings of guilt about the offence] *amongst Antillean boys, I mean boys from the Isle of Curacao.'* (GL 6)

We have made a distinction between feelings of guilt in relation to an offence and feelings of guilt in relation to the incarceration. Native Dutch boys are more likely to exhibit feelings of guilt because of the offence (five experts), while boys from ethnic minorities, especially boys of Turkish, Moroccan, and Surinamese origin, exhibit more feelings of guilt because they are incarcerated (8 experts). According to some experts, boys of Antillean origin never exhibit feelings of guilt, neither for the offence they have committed nor because of their incarceration (2 experts).
According to the experts, one reason why boys from ethnic minorities exhibit few feelings of guilt in relation to the offence they have committed is that these boys feel they are being discriminated against. This gives them a reason not to feel guilty:

> *'Young people from ethnic minorities are quick to say: 'it is because of my background, the colour of my skin, my origin; that is why we are punished so severely. (...) Even if I do have certain feelings of guilt, what difference does it make? I'm still being punished for my ethnicity.'* (GL 7)

Some of the reasons mentioned by the experts with regard to feelings of guilt that boys from ethnic minorities experience in relation to the incarceration are based on the reactions these children get from their parents about the fact of their incarceration. An expert explained the feelings of guilt suffered by boys from ethnic minorities in relation to their incarceration, and more specifically by boys of Surinamese origin, by referring to the strong bond these boys have with their mother. As another expert explained it, boys from ethnic minorities and native Dutch boys experience guilt about the incarceration in different ways. Native Dutch boys feel guilty about the fact that their parents have to come to the correctional institution (the efforts the parents have to make), whereas boys from ethnic minorities feel guilty about the loss of face suffered by the parents because their son is in custody. Two other experts explained this still further. They told us that boys from Moroccan and Turkish families, for instance, can easily suffer from feelings of guilt in relation to the incarceration because parents very clearly tell their sons that they have disgraced the family, especially when the boy in question is the eldest son. Boys from these origin groups respond to the incarceration in a way that is quite different from that of boys of Antillean origin.

Pride
Six experts observed differences in expressions of pride between ethnic origin groups. Boys of Antillean, Moroccan, and Surinamese origin, in particular, often exhibit pride more frequently than other boys. According to four of these group leaders, this pride has nothing to do with the offence or with being incarcerated in a correctional institution for juvenile offenders; boys from these minority groups show more culturally related pride.

Fear
Almost none of the experts mentioned any evidence of origin-related differences between boys who exhibit fear in the group.

4.2.3 Criminal history

Differences between 'first-time offenders' and recidivists in coping with incarceration are associated specifically with a different coping style (Mohino et al., 2004), or with the type of adjustment. Recidivists have less trouble with the practical adjustment to a custodial situation than first-time offenders (Harvey, 2007). Yet, with regard to psychological and therefore also emotional adjustment, the literature has not found any differences between the two groups (Adams, 1992; Gover et al., 2000; Harvey, 2007). The experts were asked if they observed differences in the emotions of young people who are incarcerated for the first time and young people who have already experienced an incarceration before.

Anger
Twelve experts observed a relation between previous incarceration and anger; only the experts' views differed. A number of these experts (4 of the 12) observed that boys who have previously been incarcerated will often respond in an angrier manner than first-time offenders, whereas eight experts observed the opposite.

Those experts who observed that inmates who have previously been in custody are, in fact, angrier than first-time offenders, explained their observation by telling us that the recidivists have a negative image of the police and the judicial authorities. These boys feel the police have it in for them. One expert told us:

> '*I think that they* [the recidivist] *already have negative opinions about the justice system or about society in general. Those boys are never angry with themselves, they are always angry with others, because the other has locked them up. It is possible that they are angry because they think the incarceration is undeserved. But another reason is that they think that the police are always looking for them.*' (GL 11)

Explanations that are mentioned as to why first-time offenders respond angrily more often than recidivists, relate to the person wanting to obtain a position in the group, and the lack of clarity with regard to the new situation that exists among boys who are newly incarcerated. A group leader explained:

'Everything is new to them. Being locked up, that is what they find the worst. They don't know where they are, by which I mean that everything is new and scary for them and that they still have to try to keep going. At the start, they often challenge you. (...) It is not so much anger as hostility.' (GL 4)

Some experts also tell us that recidivists are angry less often than first-time offenders because recidivists have more experience with institutions and therefore resign themselves to the situation, and know that anger does not help.

Shame

Most of the experts who occasionally observed feelings of shame in relation to the incarceration especially observed this emotion in first-time offenders (11 out of 18). This applies particularly to feelings of shame in relation to the incarceration. The reason given for these feelings of shame in first-time offenders relates to the impact of being incarcerated for the first time. Boys are often overwhelmed and do not really understand where they have ended up. These experiences induce feelings of shame. To first offenders, these feelings are specifically related to reactions of family members. It is the first time the family is told that their son is in custody. In some cases the experts observed that the boy had ended up in the correctional institution for juvenile offenders in spite of having had many warnings. Two group leaders indicated that the social environment you come from determines whether or not you will feel shame about being incarcerated in a correctional institution for juvenile offenders for the first time. As one of them stated:

'If they come from an environment where it is quite normal to have been in jail, it really is quite cool. You'll be able to talk right along with the big boys. If this is not the case, they will feel ashamed sooner, quicker. They will not know anyone in their environment who has been incarcerated.' (GL 16)

Guilt

According to those experts who observed feelings of guilt in young people, young people who experience a judicial custody for the first time feel guiltier than recidivists. This applies both to feelings of guilt in relation to the committed offence (7 out of 11), and in relation to the incarceration in a correctional institution for juvenile offenders (7 out of 19).

Why the first-time offenders are more likely to feel guilty about the committed offence than recidivists does not become clear.

The reasons the experts mentioned as to why first-time offenders are more likely to feel guilty about the incarceration than recidivists, relate to 'being roughly awakened' because they are in custody, which evokes an awareness of 'what am I doing to my parents'. In other words, the feelings of guilt surface especially as a result of what the boys are doing to their parents.

If the boys have been incarcerated before, both the boys and the parents know how everything works. There is a kind of familiarity; being incarcerated is a 'professional risk'.

Pride
Seven experts related previous contacts with judicial authorities to the exhibition of feelings of pride in the institution. According to these experts, pride about the incarceration in particular may arise from the fact that the boys have been incarcerated before. Although the experts do observe these feelings, they are not always totally clear about it. As one of them explains: 'no one is proud that he is now incarcerated for what he has done'.

Fear
Three experts observed differences between first-time offenders and recidivists with regard to the fear that boys experience in the group. According to these experts, the first-time offenders are more fearful than the recidivists are, because they are shocked about the environment in which they have ended up. This certainly applies to boys who are 'less rotten'.

4.3 Other individual characteristics

The experts also mentioned a range of background characteristics that they associate with differences in the emotional reactions of boys during custody. Because the experts were asked about background characteristics in a more general sense, they provided a broad range of answers. The background characteristics can more or less be classified into individual characteristics (cognitive, social and moral skills; personality disorders; physical characteristics); environmental characteristics (home situation and upbringing); their history (traumatic experiences); and the type of offence and sanction. It must be noted, however, that there not always is consistency, and that this section relates especially to differences that have been observed by some experts. In other words: the differences in background characteristics were not mentioned or observed by all experts. Furthermore, most experts did not provide any explanation for their observations. In the following section, we will only describe the associations the experts observed between different kinds of background characteristics and emotional reactions.

Anger
Individual characteristics that, according to the experts, are related to anger during incarceration are: a low IQ or educational sub-normality; personality disorders such as ADHD; boys with bonding problems, boys with impulse control problems; and those with so-called 'short fuses'.

Shame
The experts also observe individual differences in boys who experience feelings of shame because of the committed offence. According to the experts, the type of offence is also linked to feelings of shame. Boys who have committed a sex offence are more ashamed than other boys, according to eight experts.

Guilt
Boys who feel guilty because of the offence they have committed are characterised by their having a stronger bond with their parents (five experts), or because they have committed an offence that is low in the 'hierarchy' (robbing an elderly woman, sex offences).

Pride
According to four experts, boys with a personality disorder are more likely to feel pride in relation to the incarceration and in relation to the offence they have committed than other boys. Some other experts observe that specific types of offences are connected with pride, such as violence (four experts).

Fear
According to four experts, the background characteristics that are related to boys experiencing fear are personality disorders (depressive boys, boys with a pervasive developmental disorder not otherwise specified). However, in this context, four other experts mentioned poor social and cognitive skills (low intelligence or a negative self-image). Physical characteristics may also be connected to increased fear in boys, according to three experts. Smaller boys are more fearful than bigger boys. Three experts also linked the type of offence to feelings of fear. Boys who have committed sex offences or robbed elderly ladies will, according to these experts, respond more fearfully during their custody. One expert indicated that boys who have committed minor offences are often more fearful, because they realise they are surrounded by 'though criminals' (GW 3).

4.4 Conclusion

In this chapter, we have examined whether group leaders and behavioural scientists who are closely involved with young male inmates in their daily work observe a relation between various emotions and aspects of the (perceived) deprivation of liberty, such as being wrongfully incarcerated or the duration of the deprivation of liberty. To get a clear picture of what the experts were talking about, a description was first presented on how, according to them, the emotions manifest themselves in the boys, and how often. The experts observed the anger and fear regularly and in different

ways. The experts observed anger through, for instance, shouting, cursing, kicking or hitting, and throwing objects. They observed fear through, for example, timid behaviour, or withdrawal. The experts also observed an emotion like pride in boys in the residential group. A distinction was made between pride in relation to the offence, which is expressed in the residential group in boasting and glorifying the offence, and pride in relation to the incarceration, which is especially expressed in bragging. The experts occasionally observe this latter form of pride, but generally not very often. Overall, there was consensus among the experts about the extent to which and the way in which the emotions rage, fear, and pride in relation to the offence are observed. There was less of a consensus with regard to pride in relation to the incarceration.
We also looked at the extent to which the experts observed guilt, shame, and remorse in the boys. They rarely observe remorse. The interviews show that the distinction between feelings of shame and feelings of guilt is difficult to make. However, the experts do observe these emotions in boys in the group, albeit to a limited extent, although there certainly is no consensus among the group leaders about the extent to which these emotions occur. When the experts do observe these emotions in the boys, these are chiefly expressed during individual discussions. Here, too, a distinction is made between shame/guilt in relation to the offence, and those same emotions in relation to the incarceration. The experts observe boys being ashamed in relation to the incarceration more often than boys being ashamed because of the fact that they have committed an offence. Shame in relation to the custody is expressed, for instance, in personal discussions, and in the boys wanting to stop the interaction with their parents. According to the experts, incidences of boys feeling guilty about the offence they have committed occur infrequently, as do incidences of boys feeling guilty about the incarceration. If they do feel guilty about the offence, this is shown in the fact that they are thinking about the victim, and are willing to talk about the matter with the group leaders of their own accord.

Next, we focused on individual differences in the emotional reactions of juvenile inmates. Most experts observed no differences based on age in expressions of the emotions anger, guilt, or shame. However, some experts did observe differences in emotions between younger and older boys. However, there was no consensus among the experts as to what age group anger is observed in more often (according to some, this is the group of younger boys while, according to others, it is the group of older boys). If shame is observed at all, this is seen especially in young boys. Feelings of guilt about the offence, if observed, occur in older boys, according to the experts, and young boys are more likely to exhibit feelings of guilt in relation to the incarceration. Furthermore, feelings of pride apparently occur more frequently in older boys and feelings of fear, by contrast, in young boys.

Over half of the experts were of the opinion that hardly any differences can be seen between origin groups with regard to anger, guilt, or shame.[8] With regard to remorse and fear, no interview indicated that there are any differences based on ethnic origin group. Pride, by contrast, is an emotion that many experts link to the origin group of the young person.
Those experts who indicated that there are differences based on origin group, usually indicated that the emotions anger and shame are expressed more intensely by young people from ethnic minorities, whereas feelings of guilt are expressed more intensely by native Dutch boys. The reasons the experts gave for this phenomenon are that young people from ethnic minorities are more strongly confronted with damage to the bond with family members (the separation of family members is more intense, or they experience that family members tell them the family honour has been affected), or feel that they are being done an injustice (they feel misunderstood, get the wrong treatment, or are being slighted). The bond with family members (and more specifically the parents) is also relevant for the feelings of guilt in native Dutch boys. The fact that feelings of guilt are exhibited more by native Dutch boys is, according to the experts, caused by the strong bond these boys have with family members.

The observations of the experts regarding differences between first-time offenders and recidivists in relation to expressions of anger are not consistent. Their answers were more univocal with respect to shame, guilt, and pride. If they do observe shame or guilt, this is more likely to be in first-time offenders than in recidivists, whereas feelings of pride are observed somewhat more frequently in recidivists.

Finally, the experts referred to a number of personality and environmental characteristics that are also connected to the different emotions.

8 Here, it may be that we are looking at a bias with regard to the observation of differences based on origin, as all the experts are of native Dutch origin. The experts who do observe differences tend to have more mixed origins (native Dutch, Moroccan, and Antillean).

5 Characteristics of the custody

In this chapter, we will describe the association of emotional reactions of juvenile inmates with characteristics of the incarceration. More specifically, we will focus on experienced injustice and the phase of the custody.

5.1 The custody is perceived as undeserved

In the literature, an association is found between the perceived fairness of a sanction and emotions like anger (see Tyler, 1990; Sherman, 1993). Fairness relates to the sanction itself, for instance, someone who feels he is innocent or who feels the sanction is disproportionate to the offence. This relates to the rightfulness of a sanction. Yet, it also relates to the fairness of the treatment by those enforcing the sanction (see, for instance, Lind & Tyler, 1988; Piquero et al., 2004; Sherman, 1993; Tyler, 2003; Van der Laan, 2004). If someone feels that the sanction he has been given is undeserved, or disproportionate, or if he feels he is being treated unfairly, this may generate anger. The consequence of this anger may be that the person in question is not prepared to comply with the rules (Tyler, 1990; 2003). According to Sherman's defiance theory (1993), in some perpetrators, unacknowledged shame is at the foundation of the relation between a sanction that is perceived as unjust and anger (see also Scheff and Retzinger, 1991). According to this theory, unacknowledged shame and responding angrily instead constitute an important factor in someone's persistence in offending. In this paragraph, we will limit ourselves to the perceived undeservedness of the custody; unfair treatment is linked to the social environment, which we will look at in Chapter 6.

Nearly all of the experts (19 of the 21) indicated that there are boys who feel they do not deserve to be punished because they believe they have done nothing wrong, or they feel that the victim got what was coming to him, or they feel the custody is disproportional. Four experts even indicated that all the boys incarcerated in a custodial institution feel that they are innocent. This is linked to the phase in the penal process that the majority of the boys in a custodial institution are in. In a custodial institution, many boys are on remand. As long as someone is in this phase and has not yet been convicted by the court, officially he is not yet an offender. According to the experts, juveniles make this very clear in the group. In the interviews, the question was asked whether, according to the group leaders, being incarcerated undeservedly is related to anger or shame.

Anger

To the question to what extent perceptions about been wrongly incarcerated may be associated with angry or furious reactions, the experts had different answers. Six experts observed no connection between the perception of an undeserved custody and anger. Fifteen experts, these mainly being the group leaders, did feel that perceptions regarding the incarceration are related to with anger and observe this in some boys like, for instance, boys from ethnic minorities or boys with a low IQ. One group leader, for example, reported that boys from ethnic minorities regularly feel they have done nothing wrong and think they are only being punished because of their ethnic origin. This can cause a lot of anger. Another group leader reported that it is often the less intelligent boys in whom a link may be observed between the feeling that they are being wrongfully incarcerated and anger. These boys feel they have reacted in self-defence and therefore do not deserve to be punished at all:

> *'Often, these are the less intelligent boys. Based on their intellectual limitations, they have quite a different understanding of how things really work. For instance, a boy may think he got into a fight in which he was defending himself. The other person soon ended up in hospital and the boy in question has done nothing wrong with him at all. It then becomes clear that he has reacted disproportionately to a mere slap, in which case it was no self-defence at all. They lack this understanding. They then feel it is unfair that they are incarcerated and the other party is not.'* (GL 6)

Shame

Based on the interviews with the experts, no clear picture emerges regarding the connection between perceptions of undeserved custody and feelings of shame. Eleven of the 21 experts said that there is no relation between perceptions of undeserved custody and the expression of shame. Five experts said that there is no link, either because they observe very few feelings of shame among the boys (3 of 5), or because they think that a boy who feels he has done nothing wrong has no need to be ashamed of anything.

Seven group leaders did observe a connection between being wrongfully incarcerated and feelings of shame. These group leaders distinguished between boys who are convinced they have been wrongfully incarcerated, boys who feel they are being stigmatised, and boys who neutralise their own behaviour. In all cases, the boys are ashamed of the perceived reactions of the outside world to the fact that they are incarcerated, as this outside world is, after all, not aware of the fact that the custody is unjust.

5.2 Phase of custody

According to the literature, there is a relation between the phase of the custody and the psychological stress experienced by young people (see paragraph 3.2). Some therefore refer to the initial period of custody as a period of 'introspection' (Greve & Enzmann, 2003; Harvey, 2007), in which inmates experience emotions more strongly than during other phases of their incarceration. The longer the young people have been incarcerated, the better they adjust to the situation and strong emotional reactions are tempered.

To what extent do the experts observe a similar process with regard to the emotions anger, shame, and guilt? And what about fear, pride, or remorse? In the interviews, the experts were asked whether they had observed differences in emotions between boys who had just joined the group and boys who had been incarcerated for a longer period. In this context, it must be noted that the duration of the custody relates to the period the boys were in the groups the experts worked with. Some young people had previously been incarcerated elsewhere, and most boys had been through a period of custody in a police cell before being incarcerated in the institution.

Anger

Three experts did not observe a link between the duration of the custody and expressions of anger in young people. Sixteen experts, however, did observe a connection between the duration of the custody and anger. Within this observation, two groups may be distinguished: eight observed the anger of boys at the start of the custody, and eight experts observed expressions of anger in particular when boys have been in the group a little longer. It is remarkable that, in both cases, the experts provided similar explanations for their observation: the fact that the boys have gotten used to the new situation and have become familiar with the rules of the institution or the group in which the boys have been placed.

The experts who observed anger in particular when boys have just joined the residential group noticed that, during the early phase, the boys are exploring both the rules of the institution and the rules in the group. They push the boundaries because they are not (yet) familiar with them, which results in conflict situations. 'Pushing the boundaries' refers to testing the boundaries of the group leaders, what they can and cannot get away with, and what the rules are in the institution in question. Boys who are new to the group also test the boundaries on the part of the boys who are already in the group. According to some group leaders, gaining status constitutes an important factor in the creation of conflict situations with group leaders and in expressions of anger. According to some group leaders, the attempt to gain status within the group is also a reason for newcomers to test the boundaries of the group leaders, which results in conflict situations:

> *'Of course they are in a group with eleven boys and they talk to each other, they hear stories from the boys about how things are done here; with this group leader you can do this, with that group leader you can do that, the other group leader is more strict. The new boy will try all this out, test things.'* (GL 15)

After a while, these boys accept the situation in the custodial institution and adjust. They calm down and expressions of anger decrease:

> '*It looks like these boys* [who have been incarcerated for longer; editorial] *eventually resign themselves to their situation and because – I think – they have hit the boundaries a few times, they have a feeling of: I know what I can and can't get away with. They appear to accept their situation more readily.' (GL 8)*

In contrast to the group leaders who particularly observe anger in boys who have just joined the residential group, a proportion of group leaders felt that anger occurs especially in boys who have been in the group a bit longer. According to them, the boys need to feel safe before they will show something of their real selves. Only when they have established a bond with the group leaders and become familiar with the rules of the institution do they dare to express themselves.

Several group leaders also indicated that anger at the start of the custody is particularly related to uncertainty and a lack of clarity regarding the next stages in a boy's criminal case. This uncertainty and lack of clarity manifest themselves in anger around the times the boy's case is due to go before the court, or after the young person has talked to his lawyer. Before and after a court appearance for a criminal hearing, some boys certainly appear to experience frustration and anger. More specifically, this may be because a boy has been misbehaving during the transport to and from the courthouse and is disciplined for this behaviour. According to one group leader, during the court hearing or in a meeting with their lawyer, when boys are confronted with the length of their sanction or are told that a personality study will be conducted that may result in a PIJ measure (see Chapter 1), these are occasions that may also evoke their anger:

> *'A boy who, for instance, is incarcerated under criminal law, and finds out after thirty days what the result is, will be angry at the start but then things are clear to him. However, their stay here can be extended twice by thirty days each time. Every extension may result in anger, because they do not get the clarity they are waiting for: why can't I just go home? Why has my stay here been extended by another thirty days? (...) New anger may arise at, for instance, every new hearing, or if a boy receives a letter from a lawyer or has a meeting with a lawyer.'* (GL 11)

Shame

Four experts observed no shame at all in boys in custodial institutions. According to these experts, these boys are not ashamed, and they are certainly not ashamed because they are incarcerated.

Of the experts who did observe shame, seven did not see any connection between shame in relation to the incarceration and the duration of the deprivation of liberty. They asserted that if someone is ashamed, this is because of his personality, or it depends on the offence.
Eight experts did observe a link between shame in relation to the offence and the duration of the deprivation of liberty. If boys are ashamed of the offence or of the fact that they are incarcerated, this is expressed particularly at the start of the custody. According to six of these group leaders, the feelings of shame decrease the longer the boys are incarcerated. Reasons the experts mentioned for the presence of shame at the start of the custody are being unaccustomed, the novelty of the situation, and the unknown. Once the boys become familiar with their situation and their new impressions, the feelings of shame will eventually disappear.

Guilt
As we commented earlier, eight experts stated that feelings of guilt are hardly visible in boys in custodial institutions. This makes them wonder whether or not these boys feel guilty about what they have done or about the consequences of their deeds. This is partly because, according to the group leaders, the boys truly experience no feelings of guilt.
Of the twelve experts who believed they have observed feelings of guilt in the young people, six asserted that there is no connection between the duration of the custody and feelings of guilt.
Another proportion of the group leaders who observe feelings of guilt did feel that there is a relation between duration and guilt. In these cases, they observed feelings of guilt in particular at the start of the custody. The group leaders have the impression that boys are always more vulnerable during the first week, which enables them to zero in on how the boys feel. In the beginning, the boys experience feelings of guilt about what they have done and about the consequences of their deeds. Boys who feel guilty about the incarceration 'suddenly' realise what they have done to their loved ones. After some time, this feeling diminishes, among other reasons because the external social environment appears to have accepted that the boy is incarcerated.

Pride
With regard to pride, it is less clear whether or not there is a connection between this emotion and the duration of the deprivation of liberty. According to six experts, there is no link at all. Seven experts actually did signal a relation, but their answers did not show any consensus about exactly when pride occurs. Some observe that there are boys who come into the group with a proud, 'look at me' kind of attitude. The peers will quickly correct this behaviour, and the first signs of pride will be suppressed. Four experts observed that feelings of pride are only expressed when young people have been in the group a little longer. At the start, the boys are timid and have to get used to the group norm.

Fear

The experts observe a clear connection between the duration of the stay in custody and fear. There are individual differences, but most boys are fearful when they have just arrived in the correctional institution for juvenile offenders, and the longer they have been in the institution, the more the feelings of fear will diminish:

> *'True, they have no idea what is happening to them. You have to get undressed for this strange security inspection, open everything up, et cetera. They are definitely scared.'* (GL 16)

And another group leader reported:

> *'When boys first come into the institution, they are the most fearful. At some point, this fear disappears, although this takes longer for some than for others. On average, it takes three to four weeks before they settle down a bit here.'* (GL 2)

One reason that fear is observed, especially at the start of the custody, is the fact that it is caused by the unknown. Boys have to get used to the fact that they are incarcerated and that they have lost control over a large part of their life. According to the group leaders, feelings of fear also result from a lack of clarity. This lack of clarity relates both to the new environment and to the duration of the detention. The average time the group leaders named for the fear to disappear differed, varying from a few days to a number of weeks.

The duration of the custody and previous experiences with the judicial authorities

According to four experts, the connection between the duration of the incarceration and emotions in young people depends on previous experiences with the judicial authorities.

With regard to feelings of guilt and shame, three group leaders observed that boys who are incarcerated for the first time in particular, feel guilty or ashamed at the start of the incarceration, something they do not observe in recidivists. One expert observed:

> *'If you have never been in contact with the judicial authorities, it will have more impact on you than on those who have previously been in touch with the judicial authorities; the 'revolving door' criminals, it makes no difference to them. I would get boys in here who have been incarcerated here two, three times before; it simply doesn't matter to them. They've been there before: the building is already familiar to them, they will see the group leader: hey, how ya doing? Boys who come here for the first time do seem to wonder: where have I ended up? Sure.'* (GL 7)

5.3 Other characteristics of custody

The study also examined what other characteristics of deprivation of liberty, that were mentioned by the experts, are related to the emotions of the young people. Because we did not ask about this in a systematic manner, this is not known for all six of the emotions.
However, four experts observed a link between the regulations in an institution and anger in young people. According to these experts, the problems that the boys have with the strict regulations are accompanied by angry reactions. One expert said, for instance:

> *'Group rules. In most cases, it is considered a burden to have to comply with a number of rules that apply here that are easier to circumvent on the outside, or that are not immediately accompanied by consequences or sanctions on the outside. Here, of course, you get caught much easier. There are a number of boys who have more trouble with this, who have a 'short fuse', and who have not fully accepted the situation they find themselves in.'* (GL 9)

5.4 Conclusion

In this chapter, we examined the association experts observed between emotions and the view of young people that their incarceration is undeserved. Nearly all the experts observed young people who were of the opinion that their incarceration was undeserved. This is associated with the institutions selected for this study. In custodial institutions, there are many boys (more than one third of the population, see Chapter 1) who are still awaiting a decision about their criminal case (they are on remand), and until that time they have not yet been found guilty by court. According to some experts, it is therefore in their own best interest to maintain their innocence. The interviews show that the boys who feel they have been wrongfully incarcerated often respond more angrily to the custody than other boys. Some experts indicated that this especially occurs more frequently in boys with a low IQ and boys from ethnic minorities. A limited number of group leaders also observed a connection with shame, but this shame exists primarily because of the assumed reactions of the outside world. Boys who feel that their incarceration is undeserved, are of the opinion that they are being stigmatised as a result.

The study also looked at whether the duration of the custody is related to emotional reactions. Although not all the experts shared this view, most experts did observe that feelings of fear, shame, and guilt are expressed more strongly at the start of the custody in particular. With regard to anger, however, there was no consensus; some experts were of the opinion that anger is expressed more often at the start, whereas others observed anger more frequently in boys who have been incarcerated longer. Those group leaders who observed a connection between the duration of the custody and feelings of shame and guilt, saw these emotions more frequently in boys who had recently arrived at the institution. However, the link between the duration of the stay and emotions was not found in all the boys; most of the experts observed differences between the individual boys. These differences are associated more strongly with personality, the committed offence, or previous experiences with incarceration.

6 The social environment and emotions

In this chapter, we will describe the connection between the social environment of young people and the different emotional reactions of juveniles, as observed by the experts.

6.1 The interaction with group leaders

In the interviews, the group leaders were asked to what extent (un)fair treatment by the experts is associated with different emotions. We also asked how the experts deal with emotions on a day-to-day basis.

6.1.1 (Un)fair treatment

The study by Liebling (2006) among adult inmates, and those by Harvey (2007) and Biggam and Power (2000) among adolescent and young adult inmates all show that the way in which inmates experience and utilise social support affects their adjustment to incarceration. The study by Harvey (2007) showed that an important part of the social support offered by group leaders related to the treatment in daily interaction, and especially the extent to which someone feels he is being treated fairly. In the study by Harvey, inmates who felt they were being treated unfairly by staff members were shown to experience more psychological problems, including feelings of fear, than inmates who felt they were being treated fairly. Although this was not studied with regard to the reactions of young inmates to judicial sanctioning, the literature relating to police sanctioning in general also found that unfair treatment by those enforcing the sanction results in emotions like anger (see, for instance, Paternoster et al., 1997; Tyler, 1991). Van der Laan (2004) also found this relation among Dutch youths who had received a sanction from a police officer.
In the interviews, the experts were asked to what extent they observed that (un)fair treatment was associated to emotional reactions in juveniles. We explained that 'fair treatment' referred to a young person feeling that he was being taken seriously, or that he was being listened to.

Anger
Twelve experts observed that perceived unfair treatment may be accompanied by angry reactions from the young people. According to four experts, the anger that boys feel because they think they are being treated unfairly never lasts long 'if they are sent to their room for 10 minutes; after 10 minutes, they have completely calmed down'. (GL 11).
Eight experts added that, in this case, the anger is connected especially to the behaviour of the group leaders. Boys get angry because they feel that they are being short-changed by the group leaders (GL 8), that they are being slighted by the group leaders, that exceptions are being made to the

rules, that there is abuse of power (GW 3), or that they wrongly fail to get points when they feel they deserve them (GL 15).
Five other group leaders observed a complex interaction with the personal characteristics of the young person. If boys get angry because they feel that they are being treated unfairly by group leaders, these are boys who are easily (re)offended, who are impatient, who have difficulty expressing what is troubling them, or boys who are angry at the world at large. A female group leader observed that the anger of boys resulting from unfair treatment can be connected to the origin and gender of the group leader. According to her, boys of Turkish and Moroccan origin are always angry with female group leaders. (GL 2).

Shame
Eight experts did not see an association between (un)fair treatment by group leaders and feelings of shame in the boys. Seven experts *did* observe a relation, but according to them, shame is repressed and quickly turns into other emotions, like anger or humiliation.

Guilt
Not a single group leader observed a relation between treatment by group leaders and feelings of guilt in the boys. The behavioural scientists are less unambiguous; they suggest that unfair treatment is, in fact, related to fewer feelings of guilt.

Pride and fear
The experts observed no relation between (un)fair treatment by group leaders and emotions like pride or fear.

6.1.2 How do experts deal with emotions in practice?

In the interviews, the experts were also asked how they respond to different emotions in their daily interaction with the boys. They were asked specifically about the emotions anger, guilt, and shame.
The experts' responses may be divided into two categories: neutralisation of the emotions, or emphasising/stimulating the emotions to make the boy think more about his behaviour and the related emotions.

Anger
The experts use a similar strategy for dealing with anger in boys in custodial institutions. Anger is undesirable and may have an infectious effect on the peers. For this reason, the majority of the experts use the neutralisation strategy. This means that they first remove the young person from the group ('send him to his room') to calm down. Next, the experts will try to trace the cause of the anger in a personal discussion with the boy in question. Anger is expressed above all in the group, and is resolved by the

group leaders as much as possible as well. Behavioural scientists will only be brought in when necessary, at a later stage.

Feelings of guilt and shame in relation to the incarceration
If experts observe feelings of guilt and/or shame in boys in relation to the incarceration, a proportion of the experts said they try to neutralise the emotions (to 'reduce the level of stress'). They do this, for instance, by encouraging contact with the parents/the external social environment, by involving extra professional help, or by trying to cheer the boy up in a personal discussion. Some of the experts indicated that they actually try to stimulate the emotions in order to initiate a process of awareness.

Feelings of guilt and shame in relation to the offence
The experts take feelings of guilt and shame in relation to the offence very seriously. If the experts observe this emotion, nearly all of them said they respond in a similar manner. In a personal discussion with the boy in question, the emotions are emphasised and the experts try to use the feelings of guilt to give the young person an insight into his own behaviour (and the consequences for the victim, if there is one), stimulating the boys to learn a lesson for the future. The experts reward the young person for exhibiting these emotions; some will encourage the boy to write a letter to the victim, if there is one.

6.2 The interaction with peers

Juveniles in a custodial institution must deal with fellow group members (peers) during the day, both in a residential group and in a school setting. Peers may be of assistance in coping with the incarceration. The previously mentioned study by Harvey (2007) showed that peers are especially relevant when it comes to practical support. The literature also shows that there are group dynamics within groups of inmates that generate solidarity. These dynamics make young people stand up for each other against, for instance, the group leaders, but also encourage inmates to look after their own interests (Sykes, 1960; see also Harvey, 2007). Warr (2002) has found that the behaviour of juveniles in groups is guided by three universal mechanisms: loyalty to the group, fear of losing face in front of others, and obtaining status. According to Warr, these mechanisms are universal to groups of adolescents, and will therefore also apply to juveniles in custodial institutions.
The experts were asked to what extent they observed a relation between the interaction with fellow group members and different emotions.

Anger
A small proportion of the experts do not observe a clear link between anger and the interaction with fellow group members (3 of the 21). These experts are more likely to observe anger in the interaction with the group leaders than anger in the interaction with fellow group members. According to them, there is a feeling of 'us against the rest' among the boys.

Fifteen experts do observe a connection between the interaction with fellow group members and emotions of anger in the young people. This anger is expressed, for instance, in cursing, teasing, or challenging others. The explanations the experts came up with can be divided into two groups. Firstly, group leaders observe anger associated with fellow group members that is the result of trivial events in the interaction between the boys ('fighting over a slice of bread'), not liking each other, false accusations, insults, or a lack of appreciation for each other's situation. Secondly, 'girlfriends' or knowledge about someone's sanction may also cause anger toward fellow group members. A group leader told us:

> '*Very occasionally, you will see a small eruption happening. (...) It may be about a remote control that someone picks up just when another boy wanted to channel-surf. It is often something very minor that gets blown out of all proportion.*' (GL 8)

The group leaders also gave explanations for anger associated with fellow group members that relate particularly to obtaining and retaining one's status in the group. Every group has a 'leader, a thinker, and a doer' according to one group leader (GL 15). In the group, the boys have to 'determine their place' (GW 4; GL 15): who is the boss; what position you can grab for yourself; determining the 'pecking order'; how to hold on to your position in the group; and how to maintain your image.
As one group leader clearly put it:

'*It often happens that everything in a group escalates. (...) It is a power struggle: who is the boss, who is the boss after that, and who is the messenger boy? Often, those boys will become the boss who are a little older or who have been in custody before. The more often you have been incarcerated, the more status you will have within the group. If, as a newcomer, you think you can tell someone what to do, you are picking on the wrong guy with these boys. Often the boys are involved in certain 'deals', but that is not something we get to see. It's all about the position of power.*' (GL 5)

Anger is often vented against the weakest link (sometimes the youngest boy) in the group, which is an easy way to retain status. As one group leader stated:

'You already have a certain pecking order anyway. The boys who are a little weaker are often targeted by the stronger ones. They have to hand over part of anything they receive. When it comes to borrowing books, these boys always come last. In a boy who is at the bottom of the pecking order this may result in anger and temper fits.' (GL 9)

According to the group leaders, changes in the composition of the group, in particular, constitute moments that promote anger or rage, because then the positions in the group have to be re-determined. This refers both to situations in which a boy is new (he still has to learn the rules of the group), and to situations in which someone leaves the group, as in the following situation sketched by a group leader:

'(...) A concrete example: it happens to be a leader of the group who has left. You can see the whole group starting to think: Oh boy, who will be the new leader? Everyone is a little lost, thinking along the lines of: if I'm tough enough and if I really go against the group leaders, I can get that position for myself. This may be one of the reasons to show: I'm angry right now. It therefore is toughness in relation to other boys, I think.' (GL 15)

Shame

Three experts observed no connection between shame and the interaction with fellow group members. According to the other eighteen experts, this link does exist, but it is related to rejection by other boys, and to the type of offence.

There are boys who are ashamed because they are rejected by others and teased, for instance because of physical characteristics. These will be boys that are low in the group's pecking order. In this context, a connection is also observed with the type of offence the boys have committed. Different offences have a different status among young inmates. An offence like mugging is high on the list and will be discussed at length with fellow group members. In the case of such an offence, there actually is a lack of shame. On the other hand, there are also less 'tough' offences, such as sex offences or robbing an elderly woman. Young people who have committed these types of offences will be at the bottom of the pecking order in a correctional institution for juvenile offenders and, according to the group leaders, they will be the ones who are being teased and baited. In these boys, feelings of shame are observed that are expressed in the residential group. A group leader noted the following:

'It depends on the offence. Boys are more ashamed of sex offences and robbing old ladies.' (GL 4)

The experts did not link feelings of shame in relation to the incarceration to the interaction with fellow group members.

Guilt
Twelve of the experts did not see a relation between feelings of guilt and the interaction with fellow group members. According to these experts, feelings of guilt, both in relation to the offence and in relation to the incarceration are repressed. Showing feelings of guilt to fellow group members is considered a sign of weakness, with the risk of becoming the group's laughing stock.
Five experts did feel that there is a connection between feelings of guilt in relation to the incarceration in particular and the interaction with fellow group members. Hurtful comments from other boys about the domestic situation of a particular boy may result in feelings of guilt in the boy involved. These experts observed that boys may be made to feel guilty because they address each other about the offences they have committed. Certain young sex offenders may experience pressure when they become aware that their offence is not accepted. This may cause them to feel guilty. The experts did stress, however, that feelings of guilt are observed only in a limited number of boys.

Pride
Peers are needed to allow boys to exhibit feelings of pride. This is both pride in relation to the committed offence and pride in relation to the incarceration. Eight experts observed boys in their group who are proud of the offence they have committed. Fellow group members are important in this context. These boys express their feelings toward other boys by bragging about their offence. According to these experts, this behaviour is relevant for obtaining status in the group.
According to five experts, there are also boys who are proud of being incarcerated. These boys brag about it to their friends in the group, or tell tough stories.

Fear
According to sixteen experts, feelings of fear in boys are also connected to their interaction with fellow group members. In the view of these experts, this is related especially to both the composition of the groups (8 of the 16) and specific characteristics of individual fellow group members, such as the age of fellow group members (6 of the 16), the type of offence some fellow group members have committed (3 of the 16), and the physical condition of fellow group members (5 of the 16). Young boys (12 or 13 years old), for example, react fearfully to older boys (16 and older).

6.3 The external social environment

Is the social environment outside the institution also capable of providing support with the way in which juveniles handle custody and the emotions associated with it? Empirical literature is not very clear about this (see Chapter 3). The experts were asked whether they felt that the exhibition of the various emotions was connected to the external social environment of the young people, more specifically to family members such as parents, friends, or the professional external social environment consisting of, among others, lawyers, guardians, or probation officers.

Anger

Twelve experts indicated that it often happens that boys are angry after they have had contact with one of their parents. The reasons for this, as observed by the experts, may be divided into three groups. Firstly, two experts observed anger in boys after contact with (one of the) parents, because the parent was threatening to sever the ties with his/her child. Boys are angry because parents (for whatever reason) have threatened to cease visiting them, or because they have their son that he is no longer welcome at home.

Secondly, five experts observed that anger in boys after contact with parents is the result of their disapproval on the part of the boy's behaviour. According to these experts, these are boys who have been told by their parents that it is their own fault they are in custody, that they had previously warned the boy, or they are boys whose parents refuse to believe a 'sob story' they have come up with as an excuse. This disapproval of their behaviour may be especially threatening to boys with regard to the bond they feel with their parents.

One group leader, for example, reported the following:

> '*I don't know what the party on the other end of the telephone says, but you can tell that the boys are getting angry. It may be comments to the effect that it's the boy's own fault, that what they did was stupid, that they had been warned. To many boys, their father and mother remain important. Even when they say that it's the boy's own fault, the boys have no one left to fall back on.*' (GL 7)

Thirdly, three experts observed that the anger in boys after having had contact with their parents is evoked because the parents have shown that they do not agree either with the fact that their son has been placed in an institution, or with the institution or a person in particular. Parents pass this dissatisfaction on to their son, which then makes the boys angry when they return to the group. These parents create an 'us-them' situation and stand behind their son. They are of the opinion that the incarceration is undeserved; the parents are dissatisfied with the situation in the correctional institution for juvenile offenders, or are disgruntled that their son has not yet been released when a lawyer had promised he would be. One group leader related the following example:

> *'... not so long ago, we had two parents here, a father and a mother. The mother was very firm, protesting that 'my child is not staying in a high-security prison like this; my child does not belong here. I'm going to the media', et cetera. This boy was doing very well* [in the group; comment added by researchers], *but after he had spoken to his parents, he had an attitude of: "actually, it is wrong for me to be here".'* (GL 15)

Nine experts also observed that young people are angry after they have finished talking to their lawyer. The discussions the group leaders had about this with the boys afterward showed that the main reason for this anger is the fact that the young person involved had other expectations regarding his anticipated sentence (or the renewal of his remand) than what he was told in the meeting with the lawyer. A group leader explained it as follows:

> *'What often happens is that lawyers will initially say: in a couple of months you'll be out of here. If this "couple of months" turns into nine months, or a year, or PIJ, whatever, this results in frustrations.'* (GL 15)

The absence or unavailability of the lawyer may also cause frustration. Another group leader stated:

> *'We often see anger aimed at lawyers, especially if the lawyer is not there. The boys have to tell us in advance when they want to make a phone call. They cannot just every day grab their mobile and call whenever they want. It causes frustration and anger when the lawyer is not available to take the call, or when the lawyer did not do what the boy expected, or does not want to visit the boy.'* (GL 11)

Shame

Boys in whom the experts observe feelings of shame, show these feelings usually more intensely after contact with the parents. On rare occasions, it may also happen that a boy is ashamed after having been in contact with a guardian he has a good relationship with.

The experts observed particular a connection between the reactions of parents and feelings of shame in relation to the incarceration. The answers of the experts can be divided into two groups. On the one hand, there are the experts who think that feelings of shame after contact with parents are generated when the parents firmly disapprove of the young person's behaviour and tell him that it is his own fault he is in custody (ten experts).

On the other hand, there are five experts who indicate that feelings of shame in the young people are generated especially when the parent has told the boy what a deep impact his custody has on the life of the parent. The parent may tell the boy that he/she had to notify his school of the fact that he is in custody, or that the son has caused him/her a lot of distress. In this context, two group leaders observed feelings of shame among boys of ethnic origin, because their parents made it very clear to the boy that he had damaged the family honour.

Guilt

Feelings of guilt in relation to the committed offence are hardly ever observed. In situations in which experts did observe this emotion, it appears that parents had little to do with it.

The reactions of parents *are* relevant, however, when feelings of guilt with regard to the incarceration are concerned. In the rare cases that the experts observed feelings of guilt in relation to the incarceration, they noted that reactions from parents, in particular, play an important role in the stimulation of these feelings (17 of the 21). It is especially in cases where parents say things to their son like 'It is your own fault you are in custody' that the experts are confronted with boys who feel guilty, as in the following report from a group leader:

> '*I think that parents are the greatest factor in this. The boys will happily pick up the telephone, because they are allowed to call home. But they may put it down in great distress. You really notice it right away, but also during visiting hours, you notice it more quickly than rage, for instance. After all, boys have a certain measure of respect for their parents, which means that they are very sensitive to their opinion.*' (GL 8)

According to three experts, contact with parents only causes feelings of guilt when there is a strong bond with the parent. If no such bond exists, the reaction of a parent has no effect on the behaviour of the young person at all:

> '*We have children here who have such a troubled relationship with their parents that if the father says, for instance, "you're doing it wrong", the child will respond with "who are you to talk, I've hardly seen you in the past year".*' (GL 17)

On the other hand, parents and friends might also suppress feelings of guilt, certainly in situations in which parents feel that their son did not do anything wrong.

Four experts observed a connection between feelings of guilt about the offence and interaction with professional aid providers, such as the youth probation service and lawyers. The contact with the probation service may be associated with an awareness in the boy (according to these experts, 'sense of guilt' is too big a word). One condition for such an awareness is a good relationship between the probation officer and the boy.

According to several group leaders, comments and reactions from a lawyer, by contrast, result in a boy experiencing not more but rather fewer feelings of guilt in relation to the offence, because the lawyer focuses purely on the court case. One group leader indicated that comments from lawyers may even result in boys feeling less guilty, for instance because the lawyer has indicated that the case may be suspended or that the situation of being on remand will end pretty soon.

Pride
When we asked the experts what aspects of the external social environment engender feelings of pride in the boys, the parents were not mentioned. They did occasionally mention friends outside the institution. Yet, according to these experts, it matters much more what the status is of the young person inside the institution than that of the young person outside the institution.

Fear
The experts did not list contacts with people outside the institution as a reason for feelings of fear in the boys.

6.4 Conclusion

In this chapter, we have looked whether, according to the experts, the internal and external social environments are related to emotional reactions in the boys.

First, we investigated whether or not a relation was observed between (un) fair treatment by group leaders and emotions. The experts observed a connection between unfair treatment by group leaders and anger in boys. Most experts also shared the opinion that there is no relation between (un)fair treatment by group leaders and feelings of guilt and shame in the boys. If any feelings of guilt were observed in the young people, these were associated in particular with the offence or with the reactions of those around them. No relation was reported between (un)fair treatment and fear.

Secondly, we investigated whether the interaction with fellow group members is connected with the different emotions. The interviews showed that emotions are dependent on interactions with fellow group members. Boys exhibit anger because they want to gain or retain status. Status in the group also plays a role in expressions of pride in relation to the committed offence. According to the group leaders, boys will brag to their fellow group members about their offence, in this way confirming their status or hoping to obtain status.

According to the group leaders, feelings of guilt and shame about the offence are not exhibited because boys do not want to lose face in front of the other boys. The group leaders did, however, observe feelings of shame in young people who have little status in the group and are rejected or teased, either because of their appearance or because of the offence they have committed (sex offence or violence against, for instance, an elderly person).

In addition, other group dynamic mechanisms were observed. For instance, expressions of anger are related to a desire to protect one's own interests (for instance: obtaining slices of bread), or to rude behaviour by fellow group members (a false accusation or an insult).

Thirdly, we investigated the relation the experts observed between emotions in young people and the external social environment, such as their parents. Although the group leaders or behavioural scientists were not always present during a contact with (one of) the parents (a visit or telephone call), most experts did observe that after such a contact many boys react in a stressed manner, for instance by being angry. The reasons the experts suggested for this were the parents' disapproval of the boy's behaviour, which constitutes a threat to the boy's bond with his parents, or conversely, parents who voice their disagreement with the boy's placement in the institution, thus transferring their own anger to their son. The experts also observed that boys may come back angry after they have had a visit from a lawyer, for instance.

Although few boys exhibit feelings of guilt and shame (it is 'not done'), contacts with parents do appear to engender such feelings in some boys, according to the experts. These emotions are particularly associated with guilt and shame about the incarceration. The experts gave similar explanations for guilt and for shame. Boys are ashamed because of the disapproval of their parents, who have told the boy what impact his custody has on them, or that the boy has disgraced the family honour (especially seen in boys of ethnic origin). Disapproval from the parents also engenders feelings of guilt, for similar reasons. This makes it difficult for the experts to distinguish between the two emotions.

7 Conclusion

In this study, we investigated the relation between judicial custody and emotional reactions in juvenile inmates. Custody is a stressful process. Juveniles who do not adequately adjust to custody express this in, for example, emotional, cognitive, and behavioural problems.[9] The lack of clarity about the nearby future and uncertainty about the situation in which someone finds himself strengthen his uncertainty and emotional stress. An adequate adjustment to incarceration is characterised by acceptance of the situation in time, relatively stable, positive feelings about ones' future, and the absence of problem behaviour (a so-called equilibrium; Harvey, 2007). Inadequate adjustment to custody is characterised by persistent emotional stress, which can be followed by problem behaviour like aggression, self-harm, or (attempted) suicidal behaviour. This behaviour impedes the daily work in judicial custodial institutions and increases the probability of unsafe situations. Besides, it can be expected that an inadequate adjustment to their incarceration will reduce the learning abilities of juveniles with regard to their punishment. It will not contribute to the reduction of recidivism, either. This study focused on the emotional reactions during judicial custody in juveniles who are suspected of a criminal offence, or who have already been punished for committing a crime. The twofold central question of the study was:

- *'What is the relation between custody and the emotional reactions of juvenile inmates?*
- *And, based on the literature, what can be said about the effects of emotional reactions of juveniles during custody on criminal recidivism?'*

These central questions were further defined in four research questions, and subsequently examined on the basis of both a literature study and an empirical study. This chapter will first describe the results of both studies. Next, we will focus on the strengths and limitation of this study. Finally, we will discuss the results and formulate some recommendations for policy.

7.1 Summary of the findings

In two sub-studies, we examined the relation between custody and emotional reactions in juvenile inmates. We explored to what extent characteristics of a) the custody [sub-question 1], b) the (internal and external) social environment [sub-question 2], and c) the juvenile himself [sub-question 3] are connected to emotions during incarceration. To this effect, a literature study was conducted and interviews were held with experts who deal with young people in custodial institutions in their daily

9 It is not said that custody is a cause of these problems. These problems can be caused by other (individual) risk factors.

work. We limited the study to custody in young people in the age group from 12 to around 24. Studies that relate to interventions or treatment during custody were excluded as much as possible. In the interviews, too, our main focus was on juveniles in custody, which we maintained, for instance, by interviewing only experts who worked in juvenile correctional facilities.

7.1.1 Individual differences, characteristics of custody, and social environment: the literature

The literature study showed that little research has been done into the relation between custody and the emotional reactions of juveniles to this deprivation of liberty. Starting points were especially found in studies conducted from the stress-coping perspective. In this perspective, custody is classed as a stressful experience to which someone adjusts either adequately or inadequately. Inadequate adjustment is accompanied by strong emotional reactions and may lead to behavioural problems. With regard to juveniles, the mainly Anglo-Saxon studies focused especially on fear, but more recently, limited studies have been conducted on the connection between feelings of guilt or shame and incarceration.

Individual
First, we looked at which individual characteristics of young people are relevant for adjusting to incarceration, and at the emotions associated with them. The literature showed that, in the case of multiple problems in an individual, the levels of emotional stress and inadequate coping are higher than when such problems are lacking.

We found differences based on coping style and ethnic origin group.
- The literature (Brown & Ireland, 2005; Eftekhari et al., 2004; Ireland et al., 2005) distinguishes coping styles that are accompanied by strong emotional reactions during custody ('emotional' and 'avoidance' coping styles). Such a emotional coping styles impede an adequate adjustment to custody and, consequently, the functioning of the young person. Emotional coping styles are linked to more symptoms of depression during incarceration. Although after a period of time, changes in the coping style occur, it is not entirely clear how this happens and whether these changes take place in all young people.
- Some research showed differences between origin groups with regard to emotional reactions to custody (e.g., Adams, 1992; Gover et al., 2000; Klooster et al., 1999). Differences are found in expressions of fear, guilt, or shame.

The literature does not allow for univocal pronouncements about age differences and differences between first-time offenders or recidivists, when it comes to the emotional reactions of young people.

- Although adults and young people do appear to experience different emotions during custody, it is not clear whether there are age differences within the group of young inmates. One study found that older boys are less fearful than young boys (Gover et al., 2000), but another study found the opposite (Ireland et al., 2005).
- Some studies show that there are differences in emotional reactions during custody based on previous experiences with the judicial authorities (Gover et al., 2000), whereas other studies have found that first-time offenders and recidivists differ especially in the type of adjustment to custody and not so much in the experienced emotions (Harvey, 2007).

Custody

Secondly, we studied the relation between the characteristics of the incarceration and emotional responses. Studies among juveniles have found that the phase of the custody a juvenile is in is an important characteristic of the incarceration, which is associated with feelings of fear, guilt, or shame.

- The initial period of the custody is an emotionally stressful period, which, for many juveniles, is clearly accompanied by feelings of fear (Adams, 1992; Harvey, 2007; Mohino et al., 2004). Harvey (2007) found that, during the first days of their custody, juveniles were obsessed with their own safety and uncertain about what was going to happen; they experienced feelings like loss of control and loss of family members and friends. This uncertainty stimulates fear.
- Feelings of guilt and shame are present more strongly in this initial period than in other phases of the custody (Hosser et al., 2005).

In time, emotions that were strongly present at the start of the incarceration become less intense and occur less frequently (Harvey, 2007; Hosser et al., 2005, 2008; Ireland et al., 2001).

- The literature refers to a process of adjustment to custody that has a number of phases, ranging from no adjustment, via acceptance of the situation, to a kind of emotional and psychological balance (a so-called equilibrium). The duration of these phases is not known very well; it depends on the individuals' situation. Harvey (2007) found three phases. During the first phase, he observed intense emotional stress, while during the last phase, juvenile inmates were able to adequately deal with their custody (Harvey, 2007). They experienced, for instance, fewer (emotional) problems with rules, the absence of loved ones, or problems with fellow group members than in earlier phases. The process is fragile and juveniles can relapse into an earlier phase, for example due to the, use of drugs, or a transfer to another unit or institution.

Other characteristics of custody that, according to the literature, are related to emotional reactions in young people (especially higher levels of fear), are not participating in structured activities, having to participate in boot camps, and disciplinary sanctions that are perceived as being unjust (Gover et al., 2000). We did not find any other studies that confirmed these findings in relation to young people.

Social environment
Third, the social environment, for example social support of family, friends, staff members or peers, might be important in adjusting to the incarceration. However, with regard to juvenile inmates, the literature does not allow for univocal announcements on the association of social support with emotional responses.

7.1.2 Individual characteristics, characteristics of custody, and social environment: the experts

In interviews with the experts, – group leaders and behavioural scientists who work in judicial custodial institutions –, we asked whether they felt that specific characteristics of the custody, the social environment and individual characteristics of the young people were related to emotional reactions. We limited ourselves to asking about boys. The literature study and the empirical study took place more or less simultaneously. This means that the findings from literature studies were only used for the empirical study to a limited extent. In order to find answers to the research questions, we examined other aspects than those raised by the literature.

In the interviews, we specifically looked at the emotions anger, guilt, shame, pride, fear, and remorse. Anger, fear, and pride (about the committed offense) are emotions that the majority of the experts observed in boys in custodial institutions and which, they said, do occur regularly. Pride about being incarcerated is rarely seen. The experts only observed emotions like shame and guilt in boys in custodial institutions to a limited extent. It is difficult for the experts to observe these emotions. According to some of the experts, the two emotions are sometimes difficult to distinguish. We found too few observations of the experts with regard to remorse, which caused us to stop focusing on this emotion.

Individual
In the interviews, we asked about the extent to which there are individual differences in emotional expressions in boys during their incarceration, such as differences based on age, ethic origin, or judicial past.

- Hardly any differences based on age were observed in the various emotions, although feelings of pride (about the committed offense) occur somewhat more frequently in older boys, and feelings of fear are seen more often in younger boys.

The reasons the experts gave for the age differences with regard to emotions (irrespective of which emotion) in young boys relate particularly to the psychological distress they experience as a result of the deprivation of liberty, the 'pains of imprisonment' (see Harvey, 2007; Sykes, 1958), like uncertainty and a lack of clarity, or separation from family members. The emotions that are observed in older boys, by contrast, the experts linked to the social context of the group, such as the desire to obtain status.

- It is not clear to what extent there are differences in the expression of emotions based on ethnic origin. There was no consensus among the experts. Those experts who indicated that there are differences based on the ethnic origin group, generally stated that the emotions anger, shame, and pride are expressed more intensely by young people from ethnic minorities, whereas feelings of guilt are expressed rather more intensely by native Dutch boys. The explanations they provided for the differences in levels of rage and shame were that young people from ethnic minorities are confronted more strongly with damaged family ties (the separation from family members is more intense, or they experience how family members feel they have disgraced the family), or they feel that they are being treated unfairly (feeling misunderstood, ill-treatment, being slighted). According to the experts who mentioned this, the fact that feelings of guilt are expressed more often by native Dutch boys is because these boys have a closer bond with family members. These findings are confirmed by the literature. Fischer et al. (1999) and Mosquera et al. (2000) found cultural differences in shame, anger, and pride between cultures that valued honour (Hispanic cultures) and cultures more oriented on individual values (Dutch). In honour-related cultures, threats to someone's honour, such as threats to the family honour or being treated unjustly, will stimulate feelings of anger, whereas in cultures valuing the individual, threats to individual values, like being incarcerated or being cut off from family ties, will stimulate feelings of shame more often.
- Differences between first-time offenders and recidivists were observed especially with regard to guilt, shame, and pride. If the experts did observe shame or guilt, this was more likely to be in first-time offenders than in recidivists, whereas feelings of pride (about the committed offense) were observed rather more in recidivists. It is thinkable that feelings of shame or guilt among first-time offenders result from their awareness of the consequences of their behaviour, whereas recidivists exhibit their pride to support their status or reputation.

Custody

In the interviews with the experts, they were asked whether they had observed a relation between the various emotional reactions of young people, whether the young people considered the custody to be fair, and what their experiences were with regard to the duration of the custody and to any other characteristics of the custody.

Emotions like anger and shame seem to be related to experiences of juveniles of being unfairly incarcerated.
Nearly all experts had observed juveniles who feel they are incarcerated undeservedly. This is associated with the institutions selected for this study. Boys who are in pre-trial or on remand have not yet been found guilty by court, and in the practice of custody these boys act accordingly According to the experts, some boys are clearly convinced of their innocence. Furthermore, the experts observed boys who know that they are guilty, but think that it is in their own best interest to maintain their innocence. Both groups of boys experience their incarceration as undeserved, and respond to it more angrily than other boys in custody do.

- The anger experienced by the boys may be reinforced at the start of the incarceration as a result of uncertainty and a lack of clarity about the course of the criminal case. The experts observed anger when, for instance, the boys met with their lawyers, or when the young people returned from a court hearing where no decision had been made, but where they had heard that they would be kept in pre-trial custody longer than expected. In this context, the experts mentioned that one reason for the boys' anger is the fact that the boys had different expectations about the course of their case than materialised in meetings with their lawyer or during the court hearing. The boys would ultimately consider the pre-trial custody to be disproportional to what they had done. These findings correspond with the literature on the perceived procedural justice of sanctioning (Paternoster et al., 1997; Tyler, 1990; 2003). When people feel that the sanctioning is unjust, this might be accompanied by emotions like anger. Furthermore, empirical studies have also found a relation to rule-breaking behaviour (Paternoster et al., 1997; Tyler, 1990; 2003). In this context, it must be noted that the studies show that the treatment by those enforcing the sanction has a stronger effect on the behaviour of an inmate than the perceived fairness of the sanction. Although this study looks at the extent to which (un)fair treatment goes hand-in-hand with emotional reactions, nothing can be said about which effect is stronger.
- Some experts observed more feelings of shame in boys who experience their incarceration as being undeserved. These feelings are related to reactions of the external social environment. Juveniles who experience the sanctioning as undeserved also feel they are getting stigmatised.

The empirical study also shows that the duration of the custody is linked to emotional reactions in juveniles. However, the connection between the duration of the custody and these emotions is not found in all boys; most experts observed individual differences between the boys, which relate, among other things, to personality, the committed offence, or previous experiences with incarceration.

- Fear is expressed more strongly at the beginning of the custody. Where this was observed by the experts, this also applied to shame and guilt. These findings correspond with the literature (Harvey, 2007; Mohino et al., 2004; Hosser et al., 2005). The initial period of custody is a period that is accompanied by more intense feelings of fear, guilt, and shame, an intensity that declines as the boys have been incarcerated longer. They become more used to the limitations imposed on them and the strict rules they have to comply with (Harvey, 2007). The literature also talks about a period of 'self-reflection' (Greve & Enzmann, 2003). Although we were not looking for this, the fact that some experts observed feelings of guilt and shame more frequently in those recently arrived at the institution than in those who have been at the institution for longer, does seem to indicate a period of self-reflection. Because not all experts shared this view, it will require more specific research to more accurately determine the relation between the duration of the custody and feelings of guilt/shame.
- With regard to anger, there was no consensus: several experts felt that anger is expressed more often at the start, whereas the same number of experts observed anger more frequently in boys who have been incarcerated longer.

Social environment

- The experts observed a relation between unfair treatment by group leaders and anger in boys. These findings correspond with more general findings from literature studies regarding sanctioning: an unfair sanctioning method is linked to emotions like anger (Paternoster et al., 1997; Tyler, 1990; 2003).
- Most of the experts also shared the view that there is no connection between (un)fair treatment by group leaders and feelings of guilt and shame.
- The experts did not observe a relation between (un)fair treatment and fear, either. This does not correspond with findings from literature studies (Liebling, 2006; Harvey, 2007). It is feasible that those aspects of (un)fair treatment that were touched upon in the interviews (whether boys feel that they are being taken seriously, that they are being listened to) do not form part of the type of (un)fair treatment that is linked to feelings of fear.

The literature with regard to the interaction with fellow group members describes several group dynamic processes in custody situations, such as protecting one's own interests or prisonisation (Sykes, 1958; Harvey, 2007), processes that engender emotions like anger or pride. The experts also observe such processes in the group (for instance, anger for the purpose of protecting one's own interests). But the processes the experts especially observed can be traced back to more general group processes, such as 'status' or 'not wanting to lose face' (Warr, 2002). Therefore, these more general group processes determine the hierarchy in the group.

- A large proportion of the experts observed juveniles who want to obtain or retain status in the group. This can be achieved, among other means, by showing that you are angry, or by showing pride about the committed offence. The experts observed with some regularity that boys brag to their fellow group members about their offence, hoping to gain status or confirm their status in this way.
- Feelings of guilt and shame in relation to the committed offence are not observed. An explanation for this fact may be that boys do not want to lose face in front of other boys; they do not want to come across as being weak (see Warr, 2002). The group leaders did observe feelings of shame in young people who have little status in the group and are rejected or teased, either because of their appearance, or because of the offence they have committed. This may be a sex offence or a violent offence against an elderly person.

Although the literature is not univocal about the association of external social support with emotional reactions of juveniles in custody, the experts provided a different observation. According to them, even when juveniles are in a custodial institution, their parents still have a major impact on their emotions.

- Most of the experts observe that, after having had contact with one of the parents, many boys react in a stressed manner and are angry, for instance, or feel ashamed or guilty. Reasons that were mentioned for this anger are that the parents disapprove of their son's behaviour and that this is seen as a threat to the bond the boy has with his parents, or that parents actually show they disagree with the boy having been placed in an institution, which means that the parents' anger is transferred to the boy. The experts also observed that boys come back angry after, for instance, a visit from their lawyer.

Boys exhibit few feelings of guilt and shame, but contacts with parents do appear to engender such feelings in some boys, more specifically feelings of shame about being incarcerated.
Boys are ashamed because of their parents' disapproval when the parents have clearly told the boy what impact the custody has on them, or that the boy has disgraced the family honour (especially in boys from ethnic minorities).

7.1.3 Emotions during custody and recidivism

The fourth research question related to the connection between emotions experienced during custody and recidivism. To be able to answer this question, we used only information obtained from the literature. A few studies have been conducted in which the relation between the moral emotions anger, guilt, and shame, exhibited particularly during custody, and recidivism was explored. The studies do not present a univocal view.

- With regard to anger, it has been observed that rage during custody is not a good predictor for recidivism after the incarceration (or for misconduct during the incarceration) (see for an overview Loza-Fanous et al., 1999).
- In a study among juvenile inmates, no direct effect of feelings of guilt or shame on recidivism was found, but the study did show that, when divided into subgroups, feelings of guilt in violent delinquents are related to a reduced recidivism (Hosser et al., 2005). Because these findings are only based on a few studies, little can as yet be said about the predictive value of emotional reactions in young people during custody, when it comes to recidivism after the incarceration.

7.1.4 Possibilities and limitations of this study

In this research, the relation between custody and emotional reactions has been studied. Because on this topic only limited research has been done so far, we opted for an explorative study. The two sub-studies have both methodological possibilities and limitations. As a result of a combined systematic search strategy in several digital databases, on the basis of keywords and the snowball method, the literature study has provided us with a reasonably complete picture of today's scientific research into the way in which juvenile offenders cope emotionally with incarceration. The empirical study has provided us with insights into characteristics that, according to experts on the daily practice in correctional institutions for juvenile offenders, are related to the emotional adjustment to the deprivation of liberty. The method of a semi-structured interview offers possibilities for asking a larger group of experts the same questions, and answers to the continued questioning have clarified a range of underlying ideas about the connections between emotions and deprivation of liberty. This instrument is a suitable tool for an exploratory study when not much is known about the subject. As far as we are aware, no previous research has been done in the Netherlands into the way young detainees cope emotionally with incarceration.

One limitation of the literature study is the fact that the perception of the custody of young people with diagnosed psychiatric problems has not been taken into account. Besides, we cannot present firm conclusions about which factors are the most relevant. Studies that looked at both individual characteristics and characteristics of the custody and social environment (Adams, 1992; Gover, MacKenzie & Armstrong, 2000) show that both kinds of characteristics are associated with an adjustment to incarceration. Longitudinal research has shown that, with the passing of time, changes appear in the emotional reactions of juveniles (for example, in the type and level of fear during the initial phase as compared to later phases). Causal pronouncements in terms of effects of incarceration on emotional stress are hard to make for the moment. Thus, recent knowledge about juvenile inmates mostly focuses on the relation between incarceration and emotional stress.

Findings based on international studies cannot immediately be generalised to the Dutch context, because of differences in detention regime, the population of inmates, and cultural differences in experiencing emotions (see Chapter 1). The knowledge about the emotional stress experienced by Dutch juvenile inmates is limited.

The limitations of the empirical study relate to the selection of the expert group, the choice to interview the experts rather than the young people, and the lack of standardised questionnaires. The selection of the study group does not allow for a generalisation of the answers based on the opinions of all the group leaders and behavioural scientists in Dutch custodial institutions. Furthermore, the results relate only to the view of the experts, as the perceptions of the young people themselves were not studied. We did not use standardised questionnaires to study the incidences of emotional adjustment to custody, either. In our opinion, these limitations have had little consequence when it comes to the purpose of this study: to gain an understanding of the relation between custody and the emotional adjustment of juvenile offenders, on an exploratory basis. The aforementioned limitations would be more relevant if the objective of the study had been 'representativeness'.

During this study, it became clear that, in the context of the Netherlands, there are many gaps in the existing knowledge about the emotional reactions of juvenile offenders to custody, about which aspects are relevant in this context, and about the effect the emotional reaction to custody has on behaviour during and after the period of imprisonment. Insight into the response to custody is not only relevant in terms of the interaction and communication between professionals (group leaders, behavioural experts, lawyers, judges) and juveniles during imprisonment, but also in terms of whether or not it is possible to bring about a change in the behaviour of the young inmate. Emotional stress and negative emotions are characteristics of an inadequate adjustment to custody. They constitute an obstacle to the acceptance of treatment, whereas an adequate adjustment to custody provides opportunities for change (see, for example, Van Binsbergen, 2003). In the context of an effective approach to combating recidivism, it makes sense to obtain better insight into the manner in which young people experience their imprisonment.

Without wanting to suggest that the list provided here is exhaustive, a number of examples of 'gaps' are given below:

- In the Netherlands, no systematic research has been carried out into the mechanisms used by juvenile detainees to cope with their custody, the differences in this regard between subgroups, and the effects of coping mechanisms on their behaviour both during and after the custody. Yet, the international literature actually provides indications that some coping mechanisms are less effective than others, and that they are related to psychiatric problems amongst juveniles in the longer term. Research shows that some emotions experienced during imprisonment have an inhibiting effect on young people's willingness to change and can therefore (in addition to other individual factors) constitute a threat to the success of treatment (Van Binsbergen, 2003). It is therefore advisable to obtain a better understanding of these types of emotions and to identify the associated inadequate coping mechanisms. Zamble and Quinsey (1997) go one step further: basing themselves on the coping-relapse hypothesis, they assume that inadequate coping mechanisms during imprisonment are predictive for recidivism after the period of custody. The extent to which this applies to juveniles is not known.
- The extent to which neurobiological characteristics (or disorders) of juvenile detainees are related to their emotional reaction to imprisonment is unclear. We have not found any literature in which research has been carried out into the connection between neurobiological disorders and the emotional reactions of juvenile detainees to custody. It is to be expected that juveniles who suffer from a neurological disorder will have a different emotional response to the sanctions imposed. Research amongst groups of non-detainees has revealed, for instance, that some young people are less sensitive to sanctions involving community service or educational tasks [a so-called *Halt sanction*] as a result of neurobiological disorders (see, for example, the study carried out by Popma and Doreleijers among young people upon whom a sanction involving community service or educational tasks has been imposed).
- What role does bonding with significant others (parents, friends, members of staff, and other members of their group) play, and the juveniles' ability to develop a secure attachment in their emotional reaction to and mechanism for coping with imprisonment? And what effect does this have on their behaviour, both inside and outside of the institution? An inability to form secure attachments is a risk factor for the development of psychopathology (Koot, 1995; in Van Binsbergen, 2003) and also impedes progress during treatment (Van Binsbergen, 2003).
- Although there are differences between the emotional reactions to imprisonment amongst groups of offenders from different backgrounds, the literature currently provides little information on the emotional reaction to custody amongst different minority groups. This type of information is important in view of the composition of the population of correctional institutions for juvenile offenders.

- Little is known with regard to the effects of experienced procedural justice on the emotional reactions to custody. The international literature reveals that the experience of being treated unfairly by professionals during sanctioning is related to emotional responses, such as anxiety or anger in the short term and, in the longer term, to problem behaviour like suicide, and misbehaviour during imprisonment (Harvey, 2007; Liebling, 2006; Tyler, 2003).
- If specific groups of juvenile detainees undergo a period of introspection that fades away the longer they are in prison, the initial period of imprisonment might be a more effective period in which to intervene and to take advantage of this episode of self-reflection than later on during custody. A number of studies carried out in the UK have revealed that feelings of guilt and awareness of one's criminal behaviour during conferences between the victim and the offender could be a good indication of a lower risk of recidivism (Daly, 2005; Morris, 2002). These studies do not relate, however, to imprisonment. In the context of the development of (effective) interventions during custody, it is also important to obtain better insight into emotional reactions to custody, the way in which and the extent to which emotions occur, what changes take place and when, and which young people are affected by these changes. In this context, it is important to also take into account the fact that feelings of anxiety have often been observed at the beginning of imprisonment, and that research has shown that this emotion can have an inhibiting effect on a detainee's motivation to undergo treatment (Van Binsbergen, 2003).

7.2 Discussion and recommendations

In the Netherlands, before a juvenile offender enters a custodial institution, he has already passed through several different types of incarceration. This process starts at the police station where, after being apprehended, a juvenile offender can be held for a maximum of six hours and can be incarcerated for investigation. In many cases, underage suspects will be sent home after they have been interviewed (De Jonge & Van der Linden, 2004). However, if they are suspected of facts for which pre-trial custody is permitted,[10] the (deputy) DA may recommend police custody (to a maximum of two times three days), followed by remand in custody/imprisonment (for a maximum of 14 days; art. 63 paragraph 1 of the Code of Criminal Procedure) and/or pre-trial custody. A remand/pre-trial detention can last a maximum of 30 days and can be extended

10 As a rule, these are offences with a statutory penalty of four years or more (art. 67 of the Code of Criminal Procedure); some other offences may also qualify, such as public racism or defamation. Not having a fixed abode may also result in pre-trial custody (art. 67 paragraph 2 of the Code of Criminal Procedure).

twice (art. 66 paragraph 1 of the Code of Criminal Procedure). The pre-trial custody can be suspended at any time (subject to conditions). This may occur either at the initiative of the court or the DA, or at the request of the suspect himself (art. 80 paragraph 1 of the Code of Criminal Procedure). The pre-trial custody is terminated after a final decision has been made on the criminal case. The period the young person has been in pre-trial custody is set off against the sentence or measure imposed by the court. The police custody normally takes place at a police station, the remand in custody, and the pre-trial custody usually in a custodial institution[11] (De Jonge & Van der Linden, 2004), although the juvenile court has a lot of leeway: house arrest or night detention, for instance, are also options for realising the remand (Bartels, 2003: 117). In practice, the majority of the juveniles will stay in a custodial institution for a short period of time.

The way in which the boys experience the custody and the associated emotional reactions does not remain constant throughout the entire period of the deprivation of liberty. British research (Harvey, 2007) shows that there are a number of subsequent phases in the adjustment to incarceration, starting from a very stressful phase (with a high level of emotional stress), via acceptance of the situation, to emotional stability and adequate adjustment. This adjustment process is very fragile; boys can regress to earlier phases for all kinds of reasons. Some aspects of the custody increase the uncertainty. For professionals working with young detainees in their (daily) function, it is important to have an insight into, and understanding of, those aspects that may increase the emotional stress of these young people. This not only applies to group leaders, teachers, or behavioural experts, but also to judges and solicitors who come into contact with young suspects. In addition, emotional stress might reduce (next to other individual factors) the learning potential of juveniles with regard to behavioural change during custody. Below, we will discuss some of these aspects and, where relevant, make recommendations for practice.

7.2.1 Initial period of deprivation of liberty: an emotionally confusing time

The beginning of a custody period is an emotionally confusing time that is accompanied by shock and disbelief, irrespective of individual characteristics or the characteristics of the custodial institution. For the juvenile involved, there is considerable uncertainty about what the future holds in store, and certainly for those on remand this period is very unclear

11 In exceptional cases, namely when there is insufficient room available in custodial institutions, a suspect may also be held at a police station (art. 16a paragraph 1 and 2 of the Youth Custodial Institutions (Framework) Act) and in special circumstances, a remand in custody may take place in a prison (art. 59 paragraph 6 of the Code of Criminal Procedure).

(we will return to this later). The initial period is accompanied by (strong) feelings of fear and, (according to some studies) in the case of some young people by feelings of shame or guilt. The literature refers to a period of 'introspection' (Greve et al., 2003), in which a form of increased awareness may possibly become manifest. The emotions that are experienced at the start of this period decrease as the young person is incarcerated for a longer period of time. Some studies find a positive link between feelings of guilt experienced during deprivation of liberty, an awareness of what has been done to another person, and less (criminal) recidivism after detention (Daly, 2005; Morris, 2002).

The findings of experts in our study correspond with those in the international literature. The experts observed that in some juveniles, more specifically in first-time offenders and young suspects, feelings of guilt about what they have done are seen more often at the start of the custody than in other young people.

For the moment, our study does not provide us with sufficient certainty to say that this applies to all first-time offenders and young suspects; for this purpose, a study among young people themselves is needed.

If, in the case of specific groups of suspects, there is an initial period of introspection that fades as they are incarcerated longer, this may be a more effective period to intervene and respond to the 'awareness-raising process' than in a later phase of the custody. Some Anglo-Saxon studies show that feelings of guilt about someone's offence, evoked during restorative justice conferences, are good predictors for reduced recidivism (Daly, 2005; Morris, 2002). However, these studies do not relate to juvenile offenders in custody. In the context of developing (effective) interventions during incarceration, it is relevant to get a better insight into the emotional adjustment to custody, the way in which and the extent to which the emotions occur, in what way these emotions change during custody and when, and in which juveniles. Such findings can provide more clear-cut starting points for, for instance, the timing of training courses in which young people are stimulated to develop a greater awareness of what happened and what they have done to the victim (as is the case during a restorative justice conference). Of course, one needs to realise that other negative emotions that are present during the initial phase in prison, such as fear, can reduce the motivation of juveniles for change, among other individual risk factors. This has its consequences for the positive effects of interventions. For this reason, more research into the emotions during the initial period of incarceration in relation to the effectiveness of interventions might be useful.

Phasing of the custody?

The observation that the initial phase is emotionally confusing and therefore increases the chance of problem behaviour, raises the question how this risk should be dealt with. One possibility is to create residential groups within the custodial institutions based on phasing upon arrival (in some custodial institutions, this is already the case). The Youth Custodial Institutions (Framework) Act gives guidelines for phasing in relation to young people entering custodial institutions. To what extent these guidelines are followed by all the custodial institutions is not clear. The internal rules of one institution (Teylingereind, 2007), for instance, say that boys in the initial phase (the first week, carried over to the second week if necessary) can have limited contact with the boys in the residential group, to enable them to get used to the custodial situation.

7.2.2 Remand: lack of clarity, uncertainty and contradictory information

Most juvenile offenders start a judicial custody on remand. During this period, there is a greater or lesser level of uncertainty about the course of the criminal case and therefore also about the format and duration of the incarceration. From the point of view of criminal prosecution, remand is an important means to use optionally during the prosecution phase. As a result of placing someone in custody, it is known where the juvenile is at all times. The days the young person has been held on remand can simply be set off against any subsequent sentence. It may also be in the public interest to (temporarily) deprive young people of their liberty when a prosecution is in progress. In yet other situations, the domestic circumstances may be so dangerous that custody is the only solution for a young person to be safe (Bartels, 2003). From a legal perspective, this remand is not a penalty, but young people themselves experience custody as a punishment. A remand has its (legal and social) purpose, but it also has undesirable side effects. A substantial proportion of juvenile offenders experiences the custody as unjust, or feels that the 'punishment' is disproportional. Although this may be a form of neutralisation of their own behaviour (Sykes & Matza, 1957), this perception stimulates feelings of anger that may result in aggressive and/or rule-breaking behaviour.[12] The lack of clarity regarding the remand situation, and the fact that the juvenile does not know what is coming, both increase the uncertainty and emotional stress. This does not have a favourable effect on the safety in correctional institutions.

A preliminary residential plan during the remand period?
One option for providing more clarity about the stay in a custodial institution during the remand period is the formulation of a residential

12 External social factors that increase the emotional stress may result from meetings with solicitors, court attendances, or meetings with parents. Consider, for instance, a meeting with a solicitor, in which the young person is told that the criminal case will not have serious consequences whereas, during a court attendance not much later, the remand is extended, against all expectations. Reactions from parents who disagree with the boy's custody may also enhance feelings of anger when the boys return to the group.

plan. In situations where custody is recommended for the duration of the remand period, a residential plan can give the boy some measure of certainty about his stay in the institution. From a statutory point of view, the formulation of a residential plan is compulsory only when a young person has a remaining sentence of at least three months (BJJ), but in practice, some institutions also formulate residential plans for young people who will be in the institution for at least six weeks. Juveniles who are staying in a custodial institution on the basis of a remand, 'slip through the judicial net'. As far as we are aware, it is not common practice for custodial institutions to formulate a residential plan for juvenile offenders entering the institution on remand.

A clearly described schedule for the custody, which is formulated right at the start for every detainee, irrespective of his status, is an option for helping juveniles with the emotional adjustment to the incarceration. This may be achieved, for instance, by formulating a *preliminary* residential plan for all juvenile offenders entering a custodial institution. A preliminary residential plan upon arrival can provide a young person with more certainty about his stay. A preliminary residential plan may be based on an initial screening of the young person in question, providing the basic definition for a training-, education-, and leisure programme.
As a result of the inspection reports (Youth Inspectorate et al., 2007), the State Secretary of Justice recently emphasised in her letter to the Lower House (DJJ, 10 September 2007) that such a screening is part of a reform process for correctional institutions for juvenile offenders. Screening 'at the gate' for the purpose of formulating a preliminary residential plan, is not a task for the correctional institutions for juvenile offenders alone, but requires collaboration between different partners in the judicial chain. Information gathered from partners lower down the chain, for instance, might be used. Young people entering a correctional institution for juvenile offenders are no unknowns to the justice system. Often, they have had previous contact with Juvenile Care agencies, while most young suspects also become known at an early age to the Child Care and Protection Board, which is responsible for conducting a so-called Basic Advice Assessment (BARO). For this assessment, particular information is obtained on, for example, the functioning domains (individual, familial, the school, friends) that constitute a risk, and on whether or not, according to the assessor, there may be underlying (psychiatric) problems. Needless to say, this information must be supplemented with further information to adequately meet the needs of the young detainees; a further investigation of the young person's problems is needed as well.
Such a screening should, in our opinion, not be limited to the (criminogenic) risk factors alone, but should focus more broadly on the needs of, and the ways in which, a young person copes with stressful situations (coping styles). The literature has shown that specific coping styles of

young people increase emotional stress and therefore stimulate an inadequate adjustment to custody. An early understanding of the coping styles of young people will provide staff in correctional institutions for juvenile offenders with starting points on how to deal with specific juveniles, in order to reduce or prevent imminent emotional stress and the resulting problem behaviour (such as aggression, self-harm or (attempted) suicide). However, in the Netherlands, hardly any information is available on the way in which Dutch underage detainees cope with custody and what differences may be distinguished between the subgroups (by gender, ethnic origin, age, or underlying problems).

Perceived injustice as a result of contradictory information about the custody during the remand period

Another aspect that increases the emotional stress of young people during custody is treatment that is experienced as being unfair. This relates to the perception of the juvenile offenders in question and is therefore subjective (see also Sherman, 1993). However, for staff in custodial institutions, it is relevant to be able to recognise those situations that are perceived as being unfair for them to better understand the emotional stress of juvenile detainees. Treatment that is perceived as being unfair can increase emotional stress (anger, feelings of fear), potentially endangering the safety in a judicial institution.

One point that we feel requires attention in this context, is the contact between detainee and solicitor during the remand period. Comments from the various experts show that solicitors are not always aware of the emotional stress caused by the uncertainty of the custody during a remand period. To be told by your lawyer that your guilt has not yet been determined and that the case can be suspended soon is, although legally correct, an emotionally confusing statement for young detainees and their families, the more so if the remand is extended during the subsequent hearing. This only contributes to the conviction that the custody is unjust, and stimulates feelings of anger, for instance.

Univocal communications during the remand period?

It appears to us to be relevant that solicitors are informed about the emotional stress caused by custody during a remand period. We therefore recommend that, during the remand period, all the parties involved provide the juvenile with univocal information as much as possible. An important aspect of this information is that it is simply uncertain what the court will decide.

Alternatives for custody during remand?

Could there be alternatives for custody during remand? Dutch juvenile law does provide for the suspension of a young person's pre-trial detention on certain conditions (De Jonge & Van der Linden, 2003). In the first place, it must be noted that alternatives are not suitable for all juvenile offenders, as for instance in the case of those at risk of recidivism, or those with severe (psychiatric or psychological) problems. From a societal point of view, it is not always advisable to opt for an alternative to incarceration, either.

However, the juvenile court may decide to suspend the pre-trial detention on certain conditions and not impose custody. These conditions may be house arrest, for instance, or night detention (if the domestic situation is suitable). There are some objections attached to these alternatives, such as a heavy burden on the parents, or the impossibility to set off the house arrest against a possible custodial sentence subsequently imposed by the juvenile court (Bartels, 2003). Sometimes, this suspension is used to realise a community service order or a training order, as in the so-called 'Amsterdam hammer model' (Amsterdamse hamertjesmodel) or the 'Twente reversal' (Twentse omslag) (De Jonge & Van der Linden, 2003).[13] However, the presumption of innocence that applies during the remand period presents a problem here.

Although there are enough reasons to justify custody during the remand period, we think that custody must be used as a last resort.

7.3 In conclusion

Studies in which characteristics of an incarceration, characteristics of someone's social environment *and* individual characteristics are studied, show that aspects from all of these three areas are related both to the process of adjustment to detention and the ability to cope (emotionally and cognitively) with this detention. Following Adams (1992), we can also more or less conclude that every detainee responds differently to different situations. For an adequat adjustment to custody, it is important that the provided care is 'evidence-based', and also corresponds with the needs of the juvenile offender. The absence of Dutch empirical studies on the topic of dealing with emotions in custody limits general statements about our findings. In our view, more research with regard to juvenile experiences with incarceration is necessary.

An important finding in the literature that is supported by our empirical research is that juvenile offenders experience the initial period in custody as a very stressful time. This initial period is accompanied by emotional reactions like fear, anger, guilt, or shame. Some authors define this period as a time of 'introspection' (Greve & Enzman, 2003; Harvey, 2007). However, this emotional stress decreases the longer juveniles stay in custody.

13 In some judicial districts, the suspension of an incarceration on certain conditions is used to realise a community service order under the control of the youth probation service, but this conflicts with the presumption of innocence as, at that point, the young person has not been found guilty by the court (De Jonge & Van der Linden, 2003: 143-144).

Some aspects of incarceration can engender these emotions, along with the related problem behaviours. With regard to interaction between the juveniles and the staff members working with them, it is relevant to give univocal messages to the juveniles about their stay in custody. It is also useful to formulate a (preliminary) residential plan concerning their stay, even when a juvenile is on remand. One important recommendation, therefore, is that every custodial institution should formulate a preliminary residential plan for the young people entering the institution. This idea corresponds with the 'what works' perspective on judicial interventions, which stresses that interventions must correspond with the needs of and focus on responsiveness of detainees. Furthermore, these topics comply with today's policy intentions regarding a more accurate allocation of juvenile offenders to custodial institutions.

Literature

Adams, K. (1992). Adjusting to prison life. In M. Tonry (ed). *Crime and Justice: A review of research*. Vol. 16 (pp. 275-359). Chicago, Ill: University Press.

Bartels, A.A.J. (2003). *Jeugdstrafrecht* (Juvenile criminal law). Deventer: Kluwer.

Bereswill, M. (2004). Inside-out: Resocialisation from prison as a biographical process: A longitudinal approach to the psychodynamics of imprisonment. *Journal of Social Work Practice, 18*, 315-336.

Biggam, F.H., & Power, K.G. (1997). Social support and psychological distress in a group of incarcerated young offenders. *International Journal of Offender Therapy and Comparative Criminology, 41*, 213-230.

Binsbergen, M.H. van (2003). *Motivatie voor behandeling: Ontwikkeling van behandelmotivatie in een justitiële instelling* (Motivation for treatment). Antwerpen: Garant.

Blokland, A. (2005). *Crime over the life span: Trajectories of criminal behavior in Dutch Offenders*. Leiden: University of Leiden, dissertation.

Boendermaker, L., Bruinsma, W., Schouten, R., & Van der Pijl, M. (2006). *Met meer op één kamer? Meerpersoonskamers in de justitiële jeugdinrichtingen* (More people in one room? Multiple-person rooms in correctional institutions for juvenile offenders). Utrecht / The Hague: NIZW / WODC.

Braithwaite, J. (1989). *Crime, shame and reintegration*. Cambridge: University Press. Braithwaite, J. (2002). *Restorative justice and responsive regulation*. Oxford: University Press.

Brown, S.L., & Ireland, C.A. (2006). Coping style and distress in newly incarcerated male adolescents. *Journal of Adolescent Health, 38*, 656-661.

De Jonge, G., & Van der Linden, A.P. (2004). *Jeugd & Strafrecht: Een leer- en praktijkboek over het (internationale) jeugdstrafrecht en jeugdstrafprocesrecht* (Juvenile Law & Criminal Law. A book for study and practice on (international) juvenile criminal law and the juvenile criminal process). Deventer: Kluwer.

De Winter, M., Meijnen, M., & Goldschmidt, H.I.M. (2005). *Eindrapportage Herstelopvoeding: Een onderzoeksverslag van de pilot herstelopvoeding in JJI De Heuvelrug, locatie Eikenstein* (Final Report on Education/ Rehabilitation: A study report on the education/rehabilitation pilot study in the De Heuvelrug correctional institution for juvenile offenders, Eikenstein campus). Utrecht: University of Utrecht.

National Agency of Correctional Institutions (2007). *Capaciteit JJI per 1 april 2007 per regio, per bestemming* (The capacity in correctional institutions for juvenile offenders per 1 April 2007 per region, per destination). Ministry of Justice, The Hague, April 2007.

Eftekhari, A., Turner, A.P., & Larimer, M.E. (2004). Anger expression, coping, and substance use in adolescent offenders. *Addictive Behaviors, 29*, 1001-1008.

Ferguson, T.J., Stegge, H., Eyre, H.L., Vollmer, R., & Ashbaker, M. (2000a). Context effects and the (mal)adaptive nature of guilt and shame in children. *Genetic Social and General Psychology Monographs, 126,* 319-345.

Ferguson, T.J., Eyre, H.L., & Ashbaker, M. (2000b). Unwanted identities: A key variable in shame-anger links and gender differences in shame. *Sex Roles, 42,* 133-157.

Ferwerda, H., Van Leiden, I., Arts, N., & Hauber, A. (2006). *Halt: Het alternatief? De effecten van Halt beschreven* (HALT: The Alternative? The effects of the HALT programme described. The Hague / Arnhem: WODC / Beke Research and Consultancy Group.

Fischer, A.H., Manstead, A.S.R., & Mosquera, P.M.R. (1999). The role of honour-related vs. individualistic values in conceptualising pride, shame, and anger: Spanish and Dutch cultural prototypes. *Cognition & Emotion, 13,* 149-179.

Fischer, A.H., Mosquera, P.M.R., Van Vianen, A.E.M., & Manstead, A.S.R. (2004). Gender and culture differences in emotion. *Emotion, 4* (1), 87-94.

French, S.A., & Gendreau, P. (2006). Reducing prison misconducts. What works! *Criminal Justice and Behavior, 33,* 185-218.

Frijda, N.H. (1988). *De emoties: 'Een overzicht van onderzoek en theorie'* (The Emotions: 'An overview of research and theory'). Amsterdam: Bakker.

Gover, A.R., MacKenzie, K.L., & Armstrong, C.S. (2000). Importation and deprivation explanations of juveniles' adjustment to correctional facilities. *International Journal of Offender Therapy and Comparative Criminology, 44,* 450-467.

Greve, W., & Enzmann, D. (2003). Self-esteem maintenance among incarcerated young males: Stabilisation through accommodative processes. *International Journal of Behavioral Development, 27,* 12-20.

Greve, W., Enzmann, D., & Hosser, D. (2001). The stabilization of self-esteem among incarcerated adolescents: Accomodative and Immunizing processes. *International Journal of Offender Therapy and Comparative Criminology, 45,* 749-768.

Haidt, J. (2003). The moral emotions. In R.J. Davidson, Scherer, K.R., & Goldschmidt, H.I.M. (Eds.), *Handbook of affective sciences* (pp. 852-870). Oxford: Oxford University Press.

Harvey, J. (2007). *Young men in Prison. Surviving and adapting to life inside.* Portland, OR: Willan Publishing.

Hosser, D., Windzio, M., & Greve, W. (2005). Shame, guilt, and delinquency: A study of repeated offending with adolescent prisoners. *Zeitschrift fur Sozialpsychologie, 36,* 227-238.

Hosser, D., Windzio, M., & Greve, W. (2008). Guilt and shame as predictors of recidivism: A longitudinal study with young inmates. *Criminal Justice and Behavior, 35,* 138-152.

Hudley, C.A. (1992). Attributions for pride, anger, and guilt among incarcerated adolescents. *Criminal Justice and Behavior, 19,* 189-205.

Ireland, J.L., Boustead, R., & Ireland, C.A. (2005). Coping styles and psychological health among adolescent prisoners: A study of young and juvenile offenders. *Journal of Adolescence, 28,* 411-423.

Ireland, J.L., Brown, S.L., & Ballarini, S. (2006). Maladaptive personality traits, coping styles and psychological distress: A study of adult male prisoners. *Personality and Individual Differences, 41,* 561-573.

Jiang, S., & Fisher-Giorlando, M. (2002). Inmate misconduct: A test of the deprivation, importation, and situational models. *The Prison Journal, 82,* 335-358.

Katz, J. (1999). *How emotions work.* Chicago: The University of Chicago Press.

Klooster, E.M., Van Hoek, A.J.E., & Van 't Hoff, C.A. (1999). *Allochtonen en de strafbeleving: Een onderzoek naar de strafbeleving van Antilliaanse, Surinaamse, Marokkaanse en Turkse jongeren* (Ethnic minorities and the sanction experience: A study into the perception of penalization in Antillean, Moroccan and Turkish youths). The Hague: Prevention, Youth and Sanction Policy Department, Ministry of Justice.

Laan, A.M. van der (2004). *Weerspannigheid en delinquentie* (Defiance and delinquency). Nijmegen: Wolf Legal Publishers.

Lazarus, R. (2000). Evolution of a model of stress, coping, and discrete emotions. In V. Hill Rice (Ed.), *Handbook of stress, coping and health. Implications for nursing research, theory and practice* (pp. 195-223). Thousand Oaks: Sage.

Laub, J.H,. & Sampson, R.J. (2003). *Shared Beginnings, Divergent Lives. Delinquent Boys to Age 70.* Cambridge, MA: Harvard University Press.

Lemerise, E.A., & Dodge, K.A. (2000). The development of anger and hostile reactions. In M. Lewis & J.M. Haviland-Jones (Eds.), *Handbook of emotions* (2nd edition) (pp. 594-606). New York: The Guilford Press.

Le Sage, L. (2006). De gewetensontwikkeling van jeugdige delinquenten in diagnose en behandeling (The conscience development of juvenile delinquents in diagnosis and treatment). In L. le Sage, H. Stegge & J. Steutel (Eds.), *Jeugddelinquentie en gewetensontwikkeling: Conceptualisering, diagnostiek en behandeling* (Juvenile delinquency and conscience development. Conceptualization, diagnostics and treatment) (pp. 14-32). Amsterdam: SWP Publishers.

Le Sage, L., Stegge, H., & Steutel, J. (2006). *Jeugddelinquentie en gewetensontwikkeling: Conceptualisering, diagnostiek en behandeling* (Juvenile delinquency and conscience development: Conceptualization, diagnostics and treatment) Amsterdam: SWP Publishers.

Lewis, M. (2000). Self-conscious emotions: Embarrassment, pride, shame, and guilt. In M. Lewis & J.M. Haviland-Jones (Eds.), *Handbook of emotions* (2nd edition) (pp. 623-636). New York: Guilford Press.

Liebling, A. (1999). Prison suicide and prisoner coping. In M. Tonry & J. Petersilia (Eds.), *Prisons, Crime and Justice: An Annual Review of Research, 26,* 283-360.

Liebling, U.K.A. (2006). Prisons in transition. *International Journal of Law and Psychiatry, 29*, 422-430.
Liebling, A., & S. Maruna (2005). Introduction: The effects of imprisonment revisited. In A. Liebling & S. Maruna (Eds.), *The effects of imprisonment.* Portland, OR: Willan Publishing.
Lind, E.A., & Tyler, T.R. (1988). *The social psychology of procedural justice.* New York: Plenum Press.
Loeber, R., Slot, W., & Sergeant, J.A. (2001). *Ernstige en gewelddadige jeugddelinquentie. Omvang, oorzaken en interventies* (Serious and violent juvenile delinquency. Scope, causes and interventions). Houten: Bohn Stafleu Van Loghum.
Loeber, R., Slot, W., & Stouthamer-Loeber, M. (2006). A three-dimensional, cumulative developmental model of serious delinquency. In P.-O.H. Wikström & R.J. Sampson (Eds.), *The explanation of crime. Context, mechanisms and development* (pp. 153-194). Cambridge: Cambridge University Press.
Loza, W., & Loza-Fanous, A. (1999). Anger and prediction of violent and nonviolent offenders' recidivism. *Journal of Interpersonal Violence, 14*, 1014-1029.
Maitland, A.S., & Sluder, R.D. (1996). Victimization in prisons: A study of factors related to the general well-being of youthful inmates. *Federal Probation, 60*, 24-31.
Mascolo, M.F., & Fischer, K.W. (1995). Developmental transformations in appraisals for pride, shame, and guilt. In J.P. Tangney & K.W. Fischer (Eds.), *Self-conscious emotions* (pp. 64-114). New York: The Guilford Press.
Matkoski, S., & Verveacke, G. (2007). *Criminogene en beschermende factoren bij preventief gehechte jongens in een JJI* (Criminogenic and protective factors in boys held preventative custody in a correctional institution for juvenile offenders). Leuven / The Hague: KU Leuven / WODC (*Research and Documentation Center*).
Minister of Justice (2004). 'Jeugdsancties nieuwe stijl' ('*New style youth sanctions*'), The Hague, 28 September 2004.
Ministry of Justice (2006). *Handboek Rechtspositie jeugdigen in Justitiële Jeugdinrichtingen* (Handbook on the legal position of youths in correctional institutions for juvenile offenders). The Hague: Sdu Publishers.
Mills, J.F., & Kroner, D.G. (2003). Anger as a predictor of institutional misconduct and recidivism in a sample of violent offenders. *Journal of Interpersonal Violence, 18*, 282-294.
Mohino, S., Kirchner, T., & Forns, M. (2004). Coping strategies in young male prisoners 96. *Journal of Youth and Adolescence*, 33, 41-49.
Morris, A. (2002). Shame, guilt and remorse: Experiences from Family Group Conferences in New Zealand. In: I. Weijers & A. Duff (Eds.), *Punishing Juveniles. Principle and Critique* (pp. 157-178). Oxford: Hart Publishing.

Mosquera, P.M.R., Manstead, A.S.R., & Fischer, A.H. (2000). The role of honor-related values in the elicitation, experience, and communication of pride, shame, and anger: Spain and the Netherlands compared. *Personality and Social Psychology Bulletin 26* (7), 833-844.

Neustatter, A. (2002). *Locked in Locked Out: The experience of young offenders out of society and in prison*. London: Calouste Gulbenkian Foundation.

Novaco, R.W. (2000). Anger. In A.E. Kazdin (Ed.), *Encyclopaedia of psychology* (pp. 170-174). Washington DC: American Psychological Association.

Nurse, J., Woodcock, P., & Ormsby, J. (2003). Influence of environmental factors on mental health within prisons: focus group study 98. *British Medical Journal, 327*, 480-483.

OJJDP (2006). *Juvenile Offenders and Victims: 2006 National Report.* Washington DC: Office of Juvenile Justice and Delinquency Prevention.

Olthof, T. (2000). Shame, guilt, antisocial behavior and juvenile justice. A psychological perspective. In I. Weijers & R.A. Duff (Eds.), *Punishing Juveniles. Principles and Critique* (pp. 193-206). Oxford: Hart Publishing.

Otto, K., & Dalbert, C. (2005). Belief in a just world and its functions for young prisoners. *Journal of Research in Personality, 39*, 559-573.

Paternoster, R., Brame, R., Bachman, R., & Sherman, L.W. (1997). Do fair procedures matter? The effect of procedural justice on spouse assault. *Law & Society Review, 31*, 163-204.

Piquero, A., Gomez-Smith, Z., & Langton, L. (2004). Discerning unfairness where others may not: low self-control and unfair sanction perceptions. *Criminology, 42*, 699-733.

Sickmund, M. (2002). *Juvenile Residential Facility Census: 2000, Selected Findings*. Washington: Office of Juvenile Justice and Delinquency Prevention.

Snyder, H.N., & Sickmund, M. (2006). *Juvenile offenders and victims: 2006 National Report*. Pittsburgh: National Centre for Juvenile Justice.

Stegge, H. (2006). Emotie en gewetensvorming (*Emotion and conscience development*). In L. le Sage, H. Stegge & J. Steutel (Eds.), *Jeugddelinquentie en gewetensvorming. Conceputalisering, diagnostiek en behandeling* (Juvenile delinquency and conscience development. Conceptualization, diagnostics and treatment) (pp. 33-51). Amsterdam: SWP.

Sampson, R.J., & Laub, J.H. (1993). *Crime in the making*. Cambridge, MA: Harvard University Press.

Sampson, R.J., & Laub, J.H. (1997). A life-course theory of cumulative disadvantage and the stability of delinquency. In T.P. Thornberry (Ed.), *Developmental Theories of Crime and Delinquency. Advances in Criminological Theory*, 7 (pp. 133-161). New Brunswick: Transaction Publishers.

Scheff, T.J., & Retzinger, S.M. (1991). *Emotions and violence. Shame and rage in destructive conflicts*. Massachusetts/Toronto: Lexington.

Stokkom, B. van (2002). Moral emotions in restorative justice conferences: Managing shame, designing empathy. *Theoretical Criminology, 6,* 339-360.

Sherman, L.W. (1993). Defiance, deterrence, and irrelevance: A theory of the criminal sanction. *Journal of Research in Crime and Delinquency, 30,* 445-473.

Sykes, G. (1958). *The society of captives.* Princeton, NJ: Princeton University Press.

Sykes, G., & Messinger, S. (1960). The inmate social system. In *Theoretical studies in social organisation of the prison* (pp. 5-19). New York: Social Science Research Council.

Taylor, G. (2002). Guilt, shame and shaming. In: I. Weijers & A. Duff (Eds.), *Punishing Juveniles: Principle and Critique* (pp. 179-192). Oxford: Hart Publishing.

Tangney, J.P. (1998). How does guilt differ from shame? In J. Bybee (Ed.), *Guilt and children* (pp. 1-7). San Diego, CA: Academic Press.

Tangney, J.P. (2000a). Guilt. In A.E. Kazdin (Ed.), *Encyclopaedia of psychology* (pp. 40-42). Washington DC: American Psychological Association.

Tangney, J.P. (2000b). Shame. In A.E. Kazdin (Ed.), *Encyclopaedia of psychology* (pp. 266-269). Washington DC: American Psychological Association.

Tangney, J.P., & Fisher, K.W. (Eds.) (1995). *Self-conscious emotions: Shame, guilt, embarrassment, and pride.* New York: Guilford Press.

Tangney, J.P., Mashek, D., & Stuewig, J. (2007a). Working at the social-clinical-community-criminology interface: The George Mason University Inmate Study. *Journal of Social and Clinical Psychology, 26,* 1-21.

Tangney, J.P., Stuewig, J., & Mashek, D.J. (2007b). Moral emotions and moral behavior. *Annual Review of Psychology, 58,* 345-372.

Tibbetts, S.G. (2003). Self-conscious emotions and criminal offending. *Psychological reports, 93,* 101-126.

Toch, H., & Adams, K. (2002). *Acting Out. Maladaptive behavior in confinement.* Washington: American Psychological Association.

Tyler, T.R. (1990). *Why people obey the law.* London: Yale University Press.

Tyler, T.R. (2003). Procedural justice, legitimacy, and the effective rule of law. In M. Tonry (Ed.), *Crime and Justice. A review of research* (pp. 283-358). Chicago: University of Chicago Press.

Underwood, P.W. (2000). Social support: The promise and the reality. In V. Hill Rice (Ed.), *Handbook of stress, coping and health. Implications for nursing research, theory and practice* (pp. 367-392). Thousand Oaks: Sage.

Van Harreveld, F., Van der Pligt, J., Claassen, L., & Van Dijk, W. (2007). Inmate emotion coping and psychological and physical well-being. *Criminal Justice and Behavior, 34,* 697-708.

Warr, M. (2002). *Companions in Crime.* Cambridge: Cambridge University Press.

Wartna, B.S.J., Kalidien, S.N., Tollenaar, N., & Essers, A.A.M. (2006). Strafrechtelijke recidive van jongeren uit justitiële jeugdinrichtingen (*Criminal recidivism in young people from correctional institutions for young offenders*). The Hague: WODC. Fact sheet 2006-7.

Weerman, F.M., Bijleveld, C.C.H.J., Wijkman, M.D.S., & Van der Laan, P.H. (2006). Voortijdig schoolverlaten en criminaliteit. Een verkenning op basis van onderzoeksliteratuur en gegevens van het NSCR Schoolproject (*Dropping out of school and criminality. An exploration on the basis of data from the NSCR School Project*). Leiden: NSCR-2006-7.

Weijers, I. (2001). Een pedagogisch perspectief op het jeugdstrafrecht (*A pedagogical perspective on juvenile criminal law*). *Delikt & Delinkwent, 31*, 192-211.

Weijers, I. (2000a). *Schuld en schaamte* (Guilt and shame). Houten/Diegem: Bohn Stafleu Van Loghum.

Weijers, I. (2000b). The moral dialogue: A pedagogical perspective on juvenile justice. In I. Weijers & R.A. Duff (Eds.), *Punishing Juveniles. Principle and Critique* (pp. 135-154). Oxford: Hart Publishing.

Weijers, I. (2005) Het herstelgesprek bij jeugdige delinquenten. Sleutelteksten uit het internationale debat. Amsterdam: SWP Publishers. *(Restorative justice conferences with juvenile offenders. Key texts from the international debate).*

Weijers, I. (2007). Gaan we met het Nederlandse jeugdstrafrecht de VS achterna? (Are we following the US with regard to juvenile justice?) *Tijdschrift voor Criminologie, 49*, 170-178.

Welsh, B.C., & Farrington, D.P. (2006). Evidence-based crime prevention. In B.C. Welsh & D.P. Farrington (Eds.), *Preventing crime. What works for children, offenders, victims and places*. Dordrecht: Springer.

Wooldredge, J.D. (1999). Inmate experiences and psychological well-being. *Criminal Justice and Behavior, 26*, 235-250.

Youth Justice Board (2007). www.yjb.gov.uk/en-gb.

Zamble, E., & Porporino, F.J. (1988). *Coping, Behavior, and Adaptation in Prison Inmates*. New York: Springer Verlag.

Zamble, E., & Quinsey, V.L. (1997). *The Criminal Recidivism Process*. Cambridge: Cambridge University Press.

Appendix 1
Advisory board

Chairman

Prof. I. Weijers, PhD	Professor by Special Appointment in Juvenile Law at the Law Faculty of the University of Utrecht

Members

L. Dijkman, msc	Treatment Director at the Teijlingereind correctional institution for juvenile offenders, Ministry of Justice
G.J. Terlouw, msc	Research Coordinator of the Department for Judicial Youth Policy, Ministry of Justice

Appendix 2
Key words literature study

Custody*	Emotions*	Adjustment*
Incarceration	Anger	Coping
Sanction	Humiliation	Adjust
Probation	Fear	Adapt
Sentence	Disgust	
Punishment	Indifference	
Coercive actions	Remorse	
Penalty	Guilt	
Prison	Shame	
Inmate	Empathy	
Custody	Hope	
Imprison	Emotion	
Inmate	Pride	
Delinquent	Proud	
Offender	Revenge	
Incarcerate	Recalcitrant	
	Repent	
	Fear	

* Variants of these key words were also included in the literature search.

Appendix 3
The interview

Anger

Background characteristics

A number of questions deal with boys who respond with anger or rage more frequently than others. Other questions relate to their background characteristics. By background characteristics we mean, among other things, age, ethnicity, character traits, and diagnosed personality disorders.

1 Are there boys in the group who respond with anger or rage more frequently than others? How can you tell that these boys feel anger?
2 What are the individual background characteristics of boys who often respond with anger or rage? Could you give some examples?
3 Do boys who have previously been in contact with the judicial authorities (for instance boys who have been in custody before) respond with anger or rage more often than boys who have never been in contact with the judicial authorities before? If so, why is that? Could you give an example?
4 Do boys who newly arrive in a correctional institution respond with anger more often than boys who are there for a longer period of time? If so, why is that? Could you give an example of how this process progresses over time?

Inside the institution

5 Are there boys who feel they deserve no punishment at all because they have done nothing wrong? If so, to what extent is this accompanied by angry or furious reactions on the part of a boy? If so, why do you think this is so? Could you give an example?
Are there boys who feel the sanction they have been given is much too severe in relation to the offence for which they are in custody? If so, to what extent is this accompanied by angry or furious reactions on the part of a boy? If so, why do you think this is so? Could you give an example?
6 To what extent is the (un)fair treatment of boys by the group leaders accompanied by angry or furious reactions on the part of the boy? Why do you think this is so? Could you give an example?
7 How do you generally handle boys who respond to their punishment with anger or rage? Could you give an example?
8 To what extent is the contact with other boys in the group accompanied by angry and furious reactions on the part of a boy? Why do you think this is so? Could you give an example?
9 Is the physical environment in an institution (by this we mean the size of the rooms, the layout and architecture of the building etc.) accompanied by angry and furious reactions on the part of a boy? If so, why do you think this is so? Could you give an example?

Outside the institution

10 Are comments or reactions of family members, friends or lawyers, in other words the social environment outside the institution, accompanied by angry and furious reactions on the part of a boy regarding his punishment? If so, why do you think this is so? Could you give an example?

Guilt [Shame][14]

1 Are there boys in the group whom you know feel guilty [ashamed] about the committed offence? How can you tell that these boys feel guilty [ashamed] about the committed offence?
2 What are the background characteristics of boys who often feel guilty [ashamed] about the committed offence? Could you give some examples?
3 Do boys who have not previously been in contact with the judicial authorities feel guilty [ashamed] about the committed offence more often than boys who have previously been in contact with the judicial authorities? If so, why is that? Could you give an example?
4 Do boys who have newly arrived in a correctional institution for juvenile offenders feel guilty [ashamed] about the committed offence more often than boys who have been incarcerated longer? If so, why is that? Could you give an example?
5 Are there boys in the group whom you know feel guilty [ashamed] because they are incarcerated in a correctional institution for juvenile offenders? How can you tell that these boys feel guilty [ashamed] about their incarceration in a correctional institution for juvenile offenders?
6 What are the background characteristics of boys who often feel guilty [ashamed] because they are incarcerated in a correctional institution for juvenile offenders? Could you give some examples?
7 Do boys who have not previously been in contact with the judicial authorities feel guilty [ashamed] about their incarceration in a correctional institution for juvenile offenders more often than boys who have previously been in contact with the judicial authorities? If so, why is that? Could you give an example?
8 Do boys who have newly arrived in a correctional institution for juvenile offenders feel guilty [ashamed] about their incarceration in a correctional institution more often than boys who have been incarcerated longer? If so, why is that? Could you give an example?

14 In the interview, we first asked the questions about guilt, followed by those about shame. Because the questions are similar, here we put them together.

Inside the institution

9 To what extent is the (un)fair treatment of boys by the group leaders accompanied by feelings of guilt [shame] in the boy? Why do you think this is so? Could you give an example?

10 How do you generally handle boys who feel guilty [ashamed] about the offence they have committed? Could you give an example? How do you generally handle boys who feel guilty [ashamed] about their incarceration in a correctional institution for juvenile offenders? Could you give an example?

11 To what extent is the contact with other boys in the group accompanied by feelings of guilt [shame] in a boy? Why do you think this is so? Could you give an example?

Outside the institution

12a Are comments or reactions of family members, friends or lawyers, in other words the social environment outside the institution, accompanied by feelings of guilt [shame] on the part of a boy regarding his punishment? If so, why do you think this is so? Could you give an example?

Pride [remorse / fear][15]

1 Are there boys in the group who you know are proud of [feel remorse about] the offence they have committed? How can you tell that these boys are proud of [feel remorse about] the offence they have committed?

2 Which individual background characteristics do you observe are most often accompanied by feelings of pride [remorse / fear] on the part of the boys in relation to the committed offence?

3 Are there boys in the group who you know feel proud [remorse / fear] because they are incarcerated in a correctional institution for juvenile offenders? Can you tell that these boys feel proud [remorse / fear] of their incarceration in a correctional institution for juvenile offenders? Do boys exhibit more pride [remorse / fear] when they first arrive in a correctional institution for juvenile offenders than when they have been there for some time? If so, how does this process take place? Could you tell us something about it? If not, how do you feel this process takes place?

4 Which of the aspects of custody do you observe are most often accompanied by feelings of pride [remorse / fear] on the part of the boys in relation to their incarceration?

15 In the interview, we first asked questions about pride, followed by questions about remorse, and finally we asked questions about fear. Here, we combine these questions.

WODC-reports

In order to inform as many of those interested as possible about the research results of the WODC, a limited number of copies of the study reports are dispersed for free among officials, study groups, and institutes outside the Ministry of Justice. This is done on the basis of a mailing list, which is drawn up depending on the subject of the report concerned. The reports in the series 'Onderzoek en Beleid' (O&B - 'Research and Policy') are published by Boom Juridische uitgevers; for those not entitled to a free report, they can be ordered at Boom Distributiecentrum, postbus 400, 7940 AK Meppel, tel 0522-23 75 55, through e-mail: bdc@bdc.boom.nl. A complete list of WODC reports can be found on the WODC site (www.wodc.nl). Here, one can also find extensive summaries of all the reports published after 1997. The complete texts of the reports (published after 1999) will be made available retroactively on the WODC site. A list of the titles of the reports published since 2005 follows below.

Wartna, B.S.J., N. Tollenaar, M. Blom
Recidive 1997; Een cijfermatig overzicht van de strafrechtelijke recidive van volwassen en jeugdige daders
2005, O&B 227

Wartna, B.S.J., N. Tollenaar, A.A.M. Essers
Door na de gevangenis; Een cijfermatig overzicht van de strafrechtelijke recidive onder ex-gedetineerden
2005, O&B 228

Wartna, B.S.J., S. el Harbachi, A.M. van der Laan
Jong vast; Een cijfermatig overzicht van de strafrechtelijke recidive van ex-pupillen van justitiële jeugdinrichtingen
2005, O&B 229

Wartna, B.S.J., S. el Harbachi, L.M. van der Knaap
Buiten behandeling; Een cijfermatig overzicht van de strafrechtelijke recidive van ex-terbeschikkinggestelden
2005, O&B 230

Lünnemann, K.D., M.Y. Bruinsma
Geweld binnen en buiten; Aard, omvang en daders van huiselijk en publiek geweld in Nederland
2005, O&B 231

Erp, J.G. van, M.D. van Ewijk
Werklast bestuurlijke boete; Determinanten van de werkbelasting in de bestuursrechtspleging
2005, O&B 232

Broeksteeg, J.L.W., E.M.J. Hardy, S. Klosse, M.G.W.M. Peeters, L.F.M. Verhey
Zicht op wetgevingskwaliteit; Onderzoek naar de wetgevingsadvisering van de Raad van State
2005, O&B 233

Gritter, E., G. Knigge, N.J.M. Kwakman
De WED op de helling; Een onderzoek naar de wenselijkheid de Wet op de economische delicten te herzien
2005, O&B 234

Rovers, G.B., E. de Vries Robbé
Interne criminaliteit in de logistieke sector
2005, O&B 235

Kogel, G.H. de, V.E. den Hartogh
Contraire beëindiging van de TBS-maatregel; Aantal, aard en verband met recidive
2005, O&B 236

Eggen, A.Th.J., W. van der Heide (red.)
Criminaliteit en rechtshandhaving 2004; Ontwikkelingen en samenhangen
2006, O&B 237

Bruin, D.E. de, C.J.M. Meijerman, F.R.J. Leenders, R.V. Braam
Verslingerd aan meer dan een spel; Een onderzoek naar de aard en omvang van kansspelproblematiek in Nederland
2006, O&B 238

Knaap, L.M. van der, L.T.J. Nijssen, S. Bogaerts
Geweld verslagen? Een studie naar de preventie van geweld in het publieke en semi-publieke domein
2006, O&B 239 (239a, *Violence Defied?*)

Kogel, C.H. de, M.H. Nagtegaal, E. Neven, G. Vervaeke
Gewelddadige delinquenten met een psychische stoornis
2006, O&B 240

Martin Killias, Marcelo Fernando Aebi, Kauko Aromaa, Bruno Aubusson de Cavarlay, Gordon Barclay, Beata Gruszczyñska, Hanns von Hofer, Vasilika Hysi, Jörg - Martin Jehle, Paul Smit, Cynthia Tavares
European Sourcebook of Crime and Criminal Justice Statistics
2006, O&B 241

Faure, M.M.G., C.A.R. Moerland
Griffierechten; Een vergelijkende beschrijving van griffierechten- en vergelijkbare stelsels in een aantal landen van de Europese Unie
2006, O&B 242

Sikkel, D., P.G.M. van der Heijden, G. van Gils
Methoden voor omvangschattingen van verborgen populaties, met name illegalen
2006, O&B 243

Ferwerda, H.B., I.M.G.G. van Leiden, N.A.M. Arts, A.R. Hauber
Halt: Het Alternatief? De effecten van Halt beschreven
2006, O&B 244

Laan, A.M. van der, M. Blom
Jeugddelinquentie: risico's en bescherming; Bevindingen uit de WODC Monitor Zelfgerapporteerde Jeugdcriminaliteit 2005
2006, O&B 245

Poot, C.J. de, E.W. Kruisbergen
Kringen rond de dader; Grootschalig DNA-onderzoek als instrument in de opsporing
2006, O&B 246

Ewijk, M.D. van, M.J. ter Voert
Trendrapportage Gerechtsdeurwaarders 2006; Toegankelijkheid, continuïteit en kwaliteit van de ambtelijke dienstverlening
2006, O&B 247

Sackers, H.J.B., B.A.M. van Stokkom, J.-P. Wils
Godslastering, discriminerende uitingen wegens godsdienst en haat-uitingen; Een inventariserende studie
2007, O&B 248

Daalder, A.L.
Prostitutie in Nederland na opheffing van het bordeelverbod
2007, O&B 249

Jennissen, R.P.W. (red.), J. Oudhof (red.)
Ontwikkelingen in de maatschappelijke participatie van allochtonen
2007, O&B 250

Mheen, D. van de (red.), P. Gruter (red.)
Helingpraktijken onder de loep; Impressies van helingcircuits in Nederland
2007, O&B 251

Bunt, H.G. van de, E.R. Kleemans,
Georganiseerde criminaliteit in Nederland; Derde rapportage op basis van de Monitor Georganiseerde Criminaliteit
2007, O&B 252

Struiksma, N., J. de Ridder, H.B. Winter
De effectiviteit van bestuurlijke en strafrechtelijke milieuhandhaving
2007, O&B 253

Eshuis, R.J.J.
Het recht in betere tijden; Over de werking van interventies ter versnelling van civiele procedures
2007, O&B 254

Heide, W. van der, A.Th.J. Eggen (red.)
Criminaliteit en rechtshandhaving 2006; Ontwikkelingen en samenhangen
2007, O&B 255

Tollenaar, N., R.F. Meijer, G.L.A.M. Huijbrechts, M. Blom, S. el Harbachi
Monitor Veelplegers; Jeugdige en zeer actieve veelplegers in kaart gebracht
2007, O&B 256

Dijk, J. van, J. van Kesteren, P. Smit
Criminal Victimisation in International Perspective; Key findings from the 2004-2005 ICVS and EU ICS
2007, O&B 257

Spapens, A.C.M., H.G. van de Bunt, L. Rastovac
De wereld achter de wietteelt
2007, O&B 258

Koeter, M.W.J., M. Bakker
Effectevaluatie van de Strafrechtelijke Opvang Verslaafden (SOV)
2007, O&B 259

Kunst, M.J.J., S. Schweizer, S. Bogaerts, L.M. van der Knaap
Onderlinge agressie en geweld, posttraumatische stress en arbeidsverzuim in penitentiaire inrichtingen
2008, O&B 260 (260a, *Aggression and violence, posttraumatic stress, and absenteeism among employees in penitentiaries)*

Voert, M.J. ter, S.L. Peters
Trendrapportage advocatuur 2006; Toegankelijkheid, continuïteit en kwaliteit van de dienstverlening
2008, O&B 261

Boom, A. ten, K.F. Kuijpers, m.m.v. M.H. Moene
Behoeften van slachtoffers van delicten; Een systematische literatuurstudie naar behoeften zoals door slachtoffers zelf geuit
2008, O&B 262

Kogel, C.H. de, M.H. Nagtegaal
Toezichtprogramma's voor delinquenten en forensisch psychiatrische patiënten; Effectiviteit en veronderstelde werkzame mechanismen
2008, O&B 263

Hulst, R.C. van der, R.J.M. Neve
High-tech crime, soorten criminaliteit en hun daders; Een literatuur-inventarisatie
2008, O&B 264

Laclé, Z.D., M.J. ter Voert
Trendrapportage Notariaat 2006; Toegankelijkheid, continuïteit en kwaliteit van de dienstverlening
2008, O&B 265

Guiaux, M., A.H. Uiters, H. Wubs, E.M.Th. Beenakkers
Uitgenodigde vluchtelingen
2008, O&B 266

Klein Haarhuis, C.M., E. Niemijer
Wet en werkelijkheid; Bevindingen uit evaluaties van wetten
2008, O&B 267

Laan, A.M. van der, L. Vervoorn, C.A. van der Schans, S. Bogaerts
Ik zit vast; Een exploratieve studie naar emotionele verwerking van justitiële vrijheidsbeneming door jongeren
2008, O&B 268 (268a, *Being inside*)